Authorship, Literary Production and Censorship in the Late-Nineteenth Century

Zeynep Harputlu Shah

Authorship, Literary Production and Censorship in the Late-Nineteenth Century

Gissing-Hamsun-Halit Ziya

PETER LANG

**Bibliographic Information published by the
Deutsche Nationalbibliothek**
The Deutsche Nationalbibliothek lists this publication in the Deutsche
Nationalbibliografie; detailed bibliographic data is available online at
http://dnb.d-nb.de.

Library of Congress Cataloging-in-Publication Data
A CIP catalog record for this book has been applied for at the
Library of Congress.

Cover illustration: © maystra/istockphoto.com

ISBN 978-3-631-83800-6 (Print)
E-ISBN 978-3-631-84205-8 (E-PDF)
E-ISBN 978-3-631-84206-5 (EPUB)
E-ISBN 978-3-631-84207-2 (MOBI)
DOI 10.3726/b17849

© Peter Lang GmbH
Internationaler Verlag der Wissenschaften
Berlin 2020
All rights reserved.

Peter Lang – Berlin · Bern · Bruxelles · New York · Oxford · Warszawa · Wien

This publication has been peer reviewed.

www.peterlang.com

Contents

1. Abstract

This book provides an interdisciplinary and comparative approach to the profound transformations in the construction of authorship, literary production and censorship practices in England, Norway and the Ottoman Empire in the late nineteenth century and their influence on the representation of art and the artist in the novels of the period. Even though these countries had distinctive social, cultural, economic and political structures and conditions in the period, canonical literary works were still being produced alongside dramatic changes in the publishing and literary market and various forms of censorship being placed on art and the artist. Among the many prominent literary works, *New Grub Street* (1891) by George Gissing, *Sult* (1890) by Knut Hamsun and *Mai ve Siyah* (1896–97) by Halit Ziya Uşaklıgil stand out as essential literary works that represent the changing conditions of art and the artist in the period. The timeline of the novels (the 1890s), in particular, draws attention to the pressing need for artistic autonomy, self-expression and creativity in the novel genre. They address pivotal questions about the financial and aesthetic concerns of the novelists, the impact of (self-)censorship on their literary approach and narratives, the transforming notion of authorship, and prevailing problems in the literary and publishing world in the last decades of the century. This study argues that the novels have not only made outstanding contributions to the novel genre with their distinctive narrative style, content and form but they also exemplify the creative outcomes of implicit/explicit forms of censorships on literary production. They are innovative manifestations of the novelists challenging the dominant forms of restrictions and limitations on the freedom of expression by the artist and production of art in the period.

Keywords: authorship, literary production, (self) censorship, George Gissing, Knut Hamsun, Halit Ziya Uşaklıgil, nineteenth-century literature

2. Acknowledgements

Writing a book can be a lonely pursuit and sometimes it is difficult to see the complete picture for a long time. With the continuous support of my family, friends and colleagues, this book has been completed. I am deeply indebted to Prof. Clare Pettit and Prof. Mark Turner from King's College London for inspiring me to do some research on Victorian publishing culture and George Gissing's novels. I would also like to thank Dr Tahir Yaşar for his continuous academic support at Siirt University. I am indebted to my friends Emek Yüce Zeyrek Rios, Meral Öztürk, Sevim Güneş, and Hatice Bay for motivating me to persevere with the project. My heartfelt appreciation goes to my husband Shaheen Shah, for his constant support and advice. I would like to acknowledge with gratitude, the support and love of my parents, sisters and brothers for their understanding and patience. I am also grateful to Esra Bahşi, Padma and Suresh Selvamani from Peter Lang Publishing for their confidence in my work, patience and assistance.

3. Introduction

The primary aim of this project is to provide an interdisciplinary and comparative approach to the profound transformations in the construction of authorship, literary production and censorship practices in the late nineteenth century and their influence on the representation of art and the artist in the novels of the period. Such an outlook calls for new perspectives on the historical background and development of literary authorship and creativity, as well as the ambiguous effects of implicit and explicit forms of censorship on the artist and artistic production. Even though this project foregrounds literature, literary history and analysis, it necessarily navigates a range of disciplines among the social sciences and the humanities since literary authorship and production are deeply affected by the socio-cultural, economic and political conditions in which they are formed. For this reason, the study examines a sequence of specific contexts and concepts that shaped the conditions of literary production and the lives of the authors as they are represented in their novels.

The focus of the project is the last two decades of the nineteenth century (from 1880 to 1900) since this period represents a significant transitional era in the history of authorship, literary production and censorship, both in Europe and in the world at large. In the scholarship, a particular emphasis has been placed on specific countries, such as France, the UK, Germany, Italy and China, in certain historical periods, alongside a global perspective on authorship, literary history and censorship. However, there remains a research gap in the comparative analysis of these concepts and their impact on the literature of different countries. This project limits itself to the study of England, Norway and the Ottoman Empire in the late nineteenth century. Although these countries had distinctive social, cultural, economic and political structures and conditions in the period, canonical literary works were still being produced alongside dramatic changes in the publishing and literary market and various forms of censorship being placed on art and the artist. The strength of this study, therefore, lies in its focus on the differences and similarities among these countries regarding the specific conditions that structured late-nineteenth-century authorship and the genre of the novel.

Among the many prominent literary works in late-nineteenth-century England, Norway and the Ottoman Empire, *New Grub Street* (1891) by George Gissing, *Sult* (1890) by Knut Hamsun and *Mai ve Siyah* (1896–97) by Halit Ziya Uşaklıgil stand out as essential literary works that represent the changing conditions of art and the artist in the period. The timeline of the novels (the 1890s), in particular, draws attention to the pressing need for artistic autonomy, self-expression and creativity in the novel genre. They address pivotal questions about the financial and aesthetic concerns of the novelists, the impact of (self-)censorship on their literary approach and narratives, the transforming notion of authorship, and prevailing problems in the literary and publishing world in the last decades of the century. These questions include the following: how did the mass market, the reading public, political and/or economic concerns influence the authors' creativity and literary production? Has censorship always been a threat to authorship and artistic production? Was self-censorship an individual choice based on voluntary action or fear in the period? How and to what extent does (self-)censorship have an impact on the content, form and structure of these novels? In line with these queries, this project argues that the novels have not only made outstanding contributions to the novel genre with their distinctive narrative style, content and form but they also exemplify the creative outcomes of implicit/explicit forms of censorships on literary production. They are creative manifestations of the novelists challenging the dominant forms of restrictions and limitations on the freedom of expression by the artist and production of art in the period. A brief analysis of the city (London, Oslo, İstanbul) in the novels further provides the reader with a wider outlook on the role played by and impact of urban space on literary production and authorship, along with the pressures imposed by the public, state/governments, publishers, booksellers and editors.

This study is designed to be both general and detailed. The first chapter presents an overview of the main contexts and concepts of this project from a historical and theoretical perspective. It begins with a brief history of printing and book production and its influence on the construction and evolution of authorship and copyright, the concept and practice of censorship, and its relations with creativity and artistic production. In particular, it is noted, the invention of the printing press in the fifteenth

century triggered a dramatic transformation in book production and pro-
liferation of published materials in Europe and the rest of the world. The
concept of authorship and copyright issues also came to the fore with
technological advances in printing and publication culture, an increasing
population of reading public, and the national and international circulation of books. Along with progress in the acknowledgement of the rights of
authors and artists as the owners of their original artistic production, the
number of censorship practices over the form, content and style of intellectual creations mounted with the dissemination of published materials
among the public, as well as religious and state institutions. In this way,
authorship and literary creativity were substantially influenced by social/
public pressure, institutional censorship and self-censorship. Nevertheless,
these practices also opened up new avenues for creative production, such
as the use of camouflage, metaphors and subversion in literary works in
order to avoid possible refusals by publishers or censorship by authorities. For this reason, as this chapter argues, the influence of censorship
on authors and literary works is both complex and ambiguous since they
simultaneously restrict freedom of expression and foster authors' creativity
in various ways.

The second chapter provides the country-specific conditions of the publishing and literary culture, the transformation of authorship and copyright, and censorship practices in nineteenth-century England, Nordic
countries and the Ottoman Empire, along with their specific social, economic and political histories. Although the adoption and development of
the printing culture in these countries displayed noticeable discrepancies
from the fifteenth to the eighteenth century, the problematic condition
of literary authorship and copyright issues in the publishing world and
the practice of various forms and degrees of censorship (institutional,
public, library and publisher censors, and self-censorship etc.) remained a
locus of debate for centuries. In England, the advent of the printing press
in 1476, increasing numbers of published materials and literacy among
the public generated a literary market consisting of circulating libraries,
booksellers and publishers that held power over authors and their literary
productions. The dominant influence of the three-volume novel format
and library censors (such as Mudie's) on authors and literary production
in the nineteenth century distinguished censorship practices in England

from those in Norway and the Ottoman Empire. However, these countries had significant similarities in their censorship practices in line with the influence of public taste/opinion, publisher demands, and the prohibition of obscenity and pornographic works. Despite the absence of strict literary and press censorship legislations in England, the country had laws regarding obscenity and some anti-vice societies that attempted to preserve the moral standards of the public through campaigns.

In Nordic countries, the printing press was first introduced into Denmark in 1482 and Sweden in 1483 by Johann Snell, whilst Norway adopted it about two centuries later in 1643. The number of published works remained relatively low in Norway compared to the number of publications in Copenhagen (the literary and cultural centre of the dual monarchy) for religious and political reasons until the end of the eighteenth century. Comparably, the official adoption of the printing press by the Ottoman Empire (1727) was relatively late and close to that of Norway; however, it had already been in use by some Jewish, Armenian and Greek publishers in a lower scale from the fifteenth century. The abolition of press censorship in Denmark-Norway dates back to 1770, with some alterations and censorship practices that lasted until Norway's independence in 1814. In 1849, the freedom of the press was legalised with some limitations, including punishable acts such as false statements, obscenity and blasphemy. Not only in the literary culture of Norway and England but also in the Ottoman Empire, public opinion and publishers' demands were significant and taken into consideration in literary production and publications. However, unlike the other two countries, in the Ottoman Empire explicit forms of institutionalised censorship practices were applied to the press and literary productions. Both prior and post censorship were dominant, in particular in the last decades of the nineteenth century. For political, religious and cultural reasons, the Ottoman state had strict censorship laws in order to protect its authorial power during the decline and fall of the Empire.

The third chapter presents a detailed textual analysis of *Mai ve Siyah*, *New Grub Street* and *Sult* and the experiences of Gissing, Hamsun and Halit Ziya regarding the challenges of authorship, literary creativity, production and (self-)censorship. In this context, these narratives partly function as self-portraits of the artist as they contain some autobiographical details and focus on the changing modes of literary production in specific historical moments and cities. Gissing's naturalist realism, Hamsun's modernist approach and Halit Ziya's romantic realism present distinctive narrative techniques in dealing with the commodification of art, press and the literary market, the influence of economic and aesthetic concerns, and implicit and explicit forms of censorship on the artist and artistic production in the period. In *New Grub Street*, implicit forms of censorship, such as the reader-public's opinion and the impact of circulating libraries, publishers, reviewers and booksellers, are emphasised; in *Sult*, the editors' demands are widely shaped by public opinion on newspaper articles; and in *Mai ve Siyah*, state censorship and self-censorship play a significant role in the formation of the content and structure of the novel. Gissing, Hamsun and Halit Ziya's characterisations of the protagonists in their novels further highlight the difficulty of maintaining artistic autonomy, creativity and non-conformist attitudes against restrictive forces, such as poverty and the commercialisation of art and literature in urban space. Nevertheless, the novels themselves stand out as creative artistic productions structured by the very conditions in which they were written.

4. A Brief History of Authorship, Literary Production and Censorship

4.1 Printing and Book Production

The notion and evolution of authorship, literary production and censorship in the nineteenth century are intimately linked with the history of printing and books. From an interdisciplinary perspective, the history of books explores the life cycle of books, including production, publication, dissemination and their connection with culture, politics, economics and religion. Authors and artistic creation have long been an indispensable part of this process. In world history, book production has predominantly undergone three major transformations: the first phase was initiated with "machine printing from cast type, powered by human muscle (1455–1814)"; the second step constituted the use of "nonhuman power driving both presses and typecasting machines (1814–1970)" and the last stage has involved "computer-driven photocomposition combined with offset printing" from the 1970s to the present (Kilgour 4). The formulation of the printing press around 1440 by Johannes Gutenberg in Germany triggered a major change in book production and printing culture in the fifteenth century. With the development of the movable-type book by Gutenberg, the number of books published in Europe dramatically increased as well.[1] In the same period, centres for printing presses were established in London (1477), Rome (1467), Paris (1470) and Kraków (1473). In the following century, printing jobs remained crucial, whilst the role and importance of publishers and booksellers increased accordingly due to the connection between printed materials and the reader. With the advent of new typefaces in the sixteenth century, the significance of typography also steadily increased.

---

1 See "The Atlas of Early Printing," an interactive digital map developed by the University of Iowa displays the early history of printing in Europe during the second half of the fifteenth century.

Alongside Germany, the Netherlands became a centre for printing in Europe in the seventeenth century. By the end of the eighteenth century, printing work had become more specialised and printing houses well-established; professional illustrators, engravers, compositors and pressmen were collaborating in the printing process. The printing press transformed from muscle-powered printing to machine-powered printing during the nineteenth century. The mass production of books was widely expanded by the invention of the cast iron-type printing press by Charles Stanhope in the 1800s, the steam printing press by Friedrich Koenig in 1812, electrotyping by Mortiz con Jacobi in 1838, the rotary printing press by Richard March Hoe in 1843, the offset printing patented by Robert Barclay in 1875, and the linotype machine by Ottmar Mergenthaler in 1884. Nevertheless, the rise of mass production simultaneously caused poor production quality issues as well. Between 1860 and 1930, a number of pressmen, such as William Morris, Charles Ricketts, Thomas Cobden-Sanderson and Emery Walker, worked hard to revive quality printing through *The Arts and Crafts Movement* ("A Brief History of the Private Press Movement").

In the nineteenth century the book publishing industry in Europe grew substantially, along with an increasing number of libraries and growing literacy among the public. With mass production, for instance, a reading public of literary works began to form in the United Kingdom. Technological advances in printing further contributed to a larger number of books being published at a lower cost. Mass production, in this sense, created the necessary conditions for the generation and dissemination of contemporary literary writing and reading among the public. Publishing and marketing industries started to be global, and the roles of publishers and booksellers became more distinct and significant during the period. To illustrate, whilst writers were paid a commission based on the price and number of books sold, publishers held more power and control over the content of the books to be published.

In the UK, the printing culture accelerated the dissemination of knowledge and information among members of society and triggered an economic, social and cultural transformation (Eliot, "Aspects of the Victorian Book"). According to *Bibliotheca Londinensis*, fictional works constituted over 30 % of the total number of works published between 1814 and 1846 in the country. Book prices decreased from 1825 to 1845 and by 1855 most books were relatively affordable. In France, on the other hand, a licencing system was implemented in 1810 for booksellers in order to ensure that unwanted materials were not sold in the country. Yet despite the strict state supervision of book selling, publishers supported commercial freedom and contributed to the liberalisation of the publishing market. From the late eighteenth century to the late nineteenth century, therefore, "the literary marketplace was certainly shaped by the growth of the reading public, a rise in consumption, the development of new sources and forms of credit, the mechanisation of papermaking and printing, the invention of stereo typography and lithography, the spread of the railroad, and the institution of mass education" (Haynes 4). In the period, the publication of standardised schoolbooks, textbooks and other educational materials also resulted in the emergence of educational booksellers, and the growth of literacy and compulsory education dramatically increased the number of publishing houses across Europe.

Among the Nordic countries, the printing press was first introduced into Denmark in 1482 in Odense by Johann Snell, a German printer who printed a short prayer book *Brevarium Ottoniense* and a book entitled *De Obsidione et Bello Rhodiano* on the Turkish blockade of Rhodes Island (Ghazaryan, "The National Museum of Denmark"). In 1483, Snell also published the *Dialogus Creaturarum on Riddarholmen Island* in Stockholm, Sweden. More than a century after the advent of printing in Denmark, Sweden and Iceland (1530), Norway established its first printing house in 1643.[2] Norway and Denmark were ruled by twin monarchy in the period and Copenhagen became the centre for the literary market, book production and printing houses from 1893. By the end of the eighteenth century, there were 21 printing houses functioning in the city and only three in Norway (Dahl 19). This condition was part of the centralisation strategy of Denmark for religious and political purposes in the period. Printers, binders and sales offices constituted the publishing and dissemination institutions in early modern Norway. The first printing house in Christiania (Oslo) was established by Tyge Nielssøn in 1643 and after

---

2 In Finland, the adoption of printing was made by Peter Walde and the first print shop was established at The Royal Academy of Turku in 1640 (See Ghazaryan, "The National Museum of Denmark").

printing two theological writings he published his first book in 1644, a fortune-telling book entitled *En Ny Allmanach paa det Aar efter Jesu Christi Fødsel 1644. Christiania Aff Tyge Nielssøn* ("A New Almanac for the Year after the Birth of Jesus Christ 1644. Christiania by Tyge Nielssøn"; National Library of Norway). In the nineteenth century, the number of printing houses in Oslo remained lower than in Copenhagen.

The printed press made its first entry into the Ottoman Empire via İbrahim Müteferrika (1674–1745) about two centuries after its invention by Gutenberg in 1440 (Baykal 15). Although the method had become widespread in European countries during the sixteenth and seventeenth centuries, it was not well-established in the Empire until the eighteenth century. In fact, the printing technology was first imported into the Empire by Jewish refugees in 1493; this was followed by the establishment of an Armenian printing house in 1567, and a Greek printer set up in 1627. Since these establishments mostly relate to minorities and they were only effective in a small number of cities, Müteferrika's first publishing house and printed Ottoman-Turkish book *Vankulu Lügati* (an Arabic dictionary) in Arabic letters addressing the Turkish-speaking majority is considered the major step in the printing culture of the Empire. The official permission to establish a printing house was given by the sultan in order to supply a large number of copied books to students and major libraries. However, because of the continuous protests of manual copiers of manuscripts, who were afraid of the abolishment of their profession, the printing of religious books was avoided following an agreement between the two sides. With the first Ottoman printer, therefore, a series of history books were initially published. The number of publishing houses and printing establishments, such as *Matbaa-ı Amire* ("The Imperial Press"), also increased during this period. The reason for the delay in the advent of the printing press in the Empire was far more complex than the lack of technology.

Based on a historical and wider perspective on the emergence and dissemination of the printing press worldwide, there are a number of significant distinctions to be noted. In Europe, England followed Germany and many other countries with the advent of printing by William Caxton in 1476, whilst countries such as Norway and Finland began book publishing about two centuries later (1640). Considering the Norwegians' knowledge and use of the Danish language and the position of Copenhagen as the cultural and political centre, it can be argued that the literary market in the country was neglected until its independence from Denmark in 1814. The publication of religious texts in Norway and the increasing number of books published in Denmark leads to further obscurity in understanding the level of literacy and readership in Norway in the period. In this respect, England's records display a clearer and higher level of production and publication of literary works, as well as the size of the readership and publishing houses. In world history, the advent of printing into North America (1638–1858), South America (1539–1808), Australia (1795–1836), Africa (1494–1892), Asia (1556–1883) portrays the wide-ranging and uneven distribution of the use of the printing press on a large scale. From this perspective, the slow adoption of the printing press in the Empire does not seem to be a unique or unprecedented instance considering its particular cultural, political and religious background during the imperial decline. The dramatic increase in the production of press publications, essays, short stories and novels in the late nineteenth century confirms its final appropriation to a large extent.

Despite evident discrepancies in the emergence and development of mass printing in England, Norway and the Ottoman Empire, this revolution contributed to the generation of a new 'bookish' culture in these countries. In *Dreaming in Books* (2009), Andrew Piper notes that the nineteenth century "was a period that saw the rise of a variety of social practices and spaces cent[r]ed around the organization of books, whether it was the emergence of the public lending library, the private family library, the reading club, or the expansion of gift-giving rituals involving books" in the UK and the USA (3). This naturally made reading a significant leisure activity in private and family circles, and the suitability of a book for family reading was a quite significant factor that affected its popularity and publication. Books related to natural history and science, atlases, and travel guides were also popular among the public. However, in the nineteenth century this also led to a changing understanding of authorship and copyright issues, as well as a socially acceptable form of censorship. In the following section, the changing notion of authorship and legalisation of copyright is elaborated in connection with the history of printing and publication.

4.2 Literary Authorship and Copyright

This section introduces the concepts of authorship, the evolution of copyright and the book as intellectual property as prominent issues that developed along with the increasing numbers of printed books, dissemination of knowledge and literacy among the public within the last few centuries. Mass production, in particular, has increased the need to protect the artist and artistic productions in legal terms. As a cultural formation, "the notion of the author [...] is inseparable from the commodification of literature" (Rose 1). As a term, authorship is typically characterised by the creation of a distinct literary object and its ownership. In this sense, the author or the artist is considered both the subject and creator within the practices of the law (Saunders 128). Within the limits of the law, authors are accepted as "creative subjects [...] whose labour is legally represented as carrying the imprint of an individual personality" (128). However, contemporary theories of authorship involve an altered or re-structured interpretation of the writer "as source and centre of the text" since the literary object is considered "a structured play of forces, relations and discourses, rather than as a site of final, unified meanings, authorised by their source" (Coughie 1). Literary criticism, in this respect, often deals with "the position of the author within specific histories" and "the discursive organisation which is foundational for the text", rather than focusing on textual authority or the author "as a self-expressive individual" within the rhetoric of the text (2).

In *The Philosophy of Literature* (2009), Peter Lamarque identifies three major concepts that might help us understand the evolution of literary authorship in the nineteenth and twentieth centuries: contextualism, institutionalism and expressivism (84–5). In contextualism, a clear and concise relation is revealed between a literary text and its author. The influence of the author's life and outlook on his/her literary production is more easily interpreted by the reader or the literary critic. Institutionalism views artistic works/outcomes as products of social, cultural or political norms and traditions that reflect not only authors but also the readers and public's understandings and reactions. Expressivism, on the other hand, refers to intentional authorial control by the artist over his/her work, its originality and textual meaning. The construction of literary authorship also involves a complex set of distinctive discourses and interpretations depending on the production, publication and dissemination of artistic works, and their relations with the readership, state policies, culture, society and history. *The Cambridge Handbook of Literary Authorship* (2019) defines the concept of authorship in four distinct categories as follows:

1) the practice or activity of (literary) writing, especially of writing for publication;
2) a creative activity shaping not only words but also turning the author's life into an artistic experiment that (re-)shapes both life and work, style and man [sic]; a romantic but also classical Roman notion of authorship;
3) a form of textual control that involves cutting and taking away as well as adding: something a pair of scissors can fix; editorial and censorship practices that shape an author's work and/or image in the field of production and reception;
4) a complex of values and moral rights associated with individual creative acts in literature, such as responsibility, authority, sincerity, authenticity, which entail certain legal rights and obligations, as mandated by copyright and libel laws, such as rules for quotation and acknowledgment. (2)

Literary production solely for publication purposes serves the idea or construction of authorship as part of something commercial, cultural or institutional, which reflects an antithesis to the romantic concept of the artist, artistic freedom and creativity. The romantic view of authorship focuses on artistic creativity and originality, rather than emphasising the significance or contributions of other sources, genres or languages. The interference of commercial literary markets or publishers in literary production reduces the authorial power and makes it more difficult to find his/her self-expression in the discourse of the text. Textual control, editorial changes and censorship practices further contradict authorial independence and power. Nevertheless, situating the author as a fictional figure within a literary text might clear the way for the interpretation of the position of the author within a particular social and historical context. Intellectual works written specifically to suit the public taste, or the demands of publishers/booksellers might facilitate their reception, yet this approach will hinder authorial authenticity and self-expression. The issues of morality and the book as intellectual property are also often debated since it is argued that authorial entities and literary products "do not stand alone" and they are "socially constructed and historically contingent" (Zemer 20). In this regard, artistic/literary creation and originality in the romantic notion of authorship have frequently encountered controversies in relation to copyrighted works as "products of collective labour" in modern times (20).

Besides the literary discourse of authorship, the book as intellectual property involves an industrial capacity to produce perfect (standardised) copies, which grounds modern intellectual property law in its history (Saunders 131). Intellectual property rights stand "at the convergence of the property right (incorporeal commodity) and personality rights" (136). Michel Foucault describes the relationship between origination and proprietorship as "the solid and fundamental unit of the author and the work" (qtd in Rose 1). The names of major authors are sometimes used for "marketing cultural products" and as a sign that ensures the quality of a particular commodity (1). In cultural production, copyright as a concept refers to an individual who produces an original work and is entitled to gain profit from his/her work and efforts. Originality here refers to aesthetic creation as "the precondition of the right" and artistic creation is described in four-stages:

1) The culture or tradition has available a stock of themes or subjects from which the artist chooses. These are not invented by the artist but are available to him [sic].

2) The artist forms an imaginary representation, an initial and intentional idea of how through the work he will represent his theme in this or some possible world. This representational idea is distinguished from non-representational abstractions, such as typographic characters or, in the visual arts, a mere motif such as an arabesque. These abstractions fall below the threshold for inclusion in the category of artistic work. The imaginary representation exists entirely prior to any concrete expression.

3) The artist makes his plan or sketch, an inner form which, whilst it will be reali[s]ed in the concrete work, is independent of it.

4) The artist concreti[s]es the work in its perceptible or outer form, in which it becomes accessible to others and detachable from the artist. (Saunders 136)

In literature, both the form and content can be subject to copyright since they are artistic creations rather than scientific discoveries (137). For scientific works, on the other hand, protection is only available to representation (form) rather than the idea (content).

The earliest and most well-known copyright statute in the world was documented in England in 1710, following the *Licensing Act of 1612* in the same country. With *The Statute of Anne* (1710), the first legal act about copyright, authors were becoming "a legally empowered figure in the marketplace" as the owners of their works (Rose 4). In this way, authors, as creators of intellectual works, would gain incorporeal property rights to their work and protect their intellectual, moral and economic rights (Saunders 138). However, the issue of literary property was fundamentally a commercial struggle among booksellers, and it entailed a mixture of literary and legal discourses with a collection of texts, such as pamphlets, parliamentary records and legal reports in eighteenth-century England (Rose 4–6). One of the main concerns about these laws related to regulating book trade in order to diminish the chaos generated by the booksellers' monopoly by the end of the seventeenth century (Saunders 138). In this respect, the English copyright law not only allowed authors but also corporate entities, to be right-holders and to exercise "commercial calculations", rather than the principle of "an individual's creative act" (138). *The Statue of Anne* granted a limited period of copyright and was subject to expiration after 14 years. Nevertheless, as Annabel Patterson suggests, English copyright also meant that:

> [C]opyright would henceforth be a concept embracing all the rights that an author might have in his [sic] published work. And since copyright was still available to the publisher, its change meant also that the publisher as copyright owner would have the same rights as the author. Copyright, in short, was to become a concept to embrace all the rights to be had in connection with published works, either by the author or the publisher. As such, it was to prevent a recognition of the different interests of the two, and thus preclude the development of a satisfactory law to protect the interests of the author as author. (151)

However, the disagreements among publishers and booksellers, and their monopoly in England, continued until the introduction of the *Copyright Act of 1842*. This act granted authors lifetime protection of their literary and artistic works and remained in force until the *Copyright Act of 1911*. The United States issued its copyright legislation, the *Copyright Act of 1790*, about 80 years after *the Statue of Anne*. The first lawsuit adopted concerning copyright in the country was *Wheaton v Peters* in

1814. These copyright legislations did not reach an international level until the nineteenth century. *The Berne Convention* in 1886 provided nation states with a mutual recognition of copyright and contributed to the development of international standards for worldwide copyright protection. The Convention has been adopted by over 140 states around the world, including Scandinavian countries (Denmark, Norway, Sweden, Finland and Iceland) and the United States, and it is still a fundamental international copyright law.

Long after the advent of the printing press in the fifteenth century, the first document that confirmed copyright for writers in the Ottoman Empire was issued during the Tanzimat era ("Modernisation Period") with the *Statue of Ercümen-i Daniş* ("The Privy Council", 1851–1862) (Güher Erer 642). In 1857, *Matbaalar Nizamnamesi* ("Regulation of the Press") aimed to regulate and supervise printing houses through censorship practices and at the same time it provided authors with lifelong copyright protection. Within the Islamic law of the Ottoman Empire, the concept of copyright was recognised; however, it was not a tangible commodity and could not be purchased. The secular legal system (based on the French law) adopted by the Empire during the Tanzimat era introduced a re-interpretation of the transferability of copyright, as in European countries. The development of printing, therefore, introduced literary circles to "a new type of market, a new type of commercial organisation, a new type of legal norm and, thereby, a new type of creator" (qtd in Saunders 141). Copyright laws displayed the convergence of legal and literary histories, in the recognition and protection of personal and intellectual property rights in literature, both in Europe and in the Ottoman Empire. In the following section, literary censorship will be examined by considering the legal relations of literary studies from an antithetic perspective.

4.3 Censorship: A Historical and Theoretical Outlook

The long history of censorship is closely linked with the histories of printing, literary authorship and production, as well as copyright practices. Although the term "censor" originates from the censor office established in Rome in 443 BC, its application in practice can be traced back to the Sumerian, Egyptian, Greek and Chinese communities (Newth, "The Long History of Censorship"). In Europe, the invention of the printing press in the fifteenth century substantially increased various forms and practices of censorship. Censorship and religious matters first came to the forefront with the clash between the Catholic Church and the Protestant Reformation in the period. In line with the acceptance of the *Index Librorum Prohibitorum* ("The Index of Prohibited Books") in particular, a large number of listed books were prohibited in 1550 by Pope Paul IV. This list was issued about 20 times, until its last issue that appeared in 1948, and it was finally abolished in 1966. During the sixteenth and seventeenth centuries, books were banned and burned for their unwanted content and some famous authors such as Galileo (1633) and Thomas More (1535) were censored. Censorship applied by the Catholic Church in the printing and sale of books in 1543 were followed by the control and permission of the King of France in 1563. European rulers issued printing licences in order to protect the established social and political order.

In nineteenth-century Europe, censorship practices on literature and art included prior and post censors on a wide range of materials, such as books, plays, caricatures, opera, maps, paintings and even specific words. The circulation of information among the public was also restricted through political censorship on the opposing press through post mails and newspapers. As political, economic, moral, socio-cultural and religious censorship constrained the circulation of opinions and artistic creation, many writers, artists and activists struggled to find alternative ways to publicise and disseminate their works (Goldstein 1). The concept of the nation state was also becoming critical in the period and new political movements such as socialism emerged as a threat to the state authorities in Europe. Freedom of expression and new legislation against censorship were being demanded. Advances in the printing press technology after the 1870s, more affordable published materials, and the increasing rate of literacy all contributed to the emergence of a mass reading public. Newspapers, in particular, played a critical role in informing the public and became a modern mass agent in the period. The boundaries of censorship and freedom were also tested by a number of groups, such as anarchists, journalists, pornographers and communists, benefiting from the printing press and using literature or newspapers for the dissemination of their opinions. Some countries in Europe used legal prosecution (Netherlands), while others (Germany) introduced new laws and legislation in order to cope with unwelcome groups. Religious divisions were another factor threatening the existence of freedom of speech for particular groups, such as Jews in Eastern Europe.

From the sixteenth to the nineteenth century, the expansion of mass printing and the reading public contributed to creating a social and cultural practice organised around books, which determined the suitability of certain books for family reading, gifts and libraries, and influenced their popularity and publication. Not only poetry books, short stories and novels but also atlases, travel guides and books related to science and nature were popular among the readership. This understanding in the United Kingdom and United States, in particular, resulted in a form of social censorship of literary works that proved to be "more repressive than overt state or church power" (Foerstel xvi). During the mid and late nineteenth century, not only propriety, prudence and sexual restraint but also concerns about public virtue forced publishers, editors, authors and librarians to inspect books for "crude language or unduly explicit or realistic portrayals of life" (xvi). To ensure suitability for family reading, for instance, some "offensive" elements or "inappropriate" passages would be removed from the text. In 1818, for instance, Thomas Bowdler (1754–1825) published *The Family Shakespeare* with alterations such as the replacement of Lady Macbeth's "Out, damned spot!" with "Heavens!" and the substitution of Ophelia's suicide with accidental drowning. Book burning for religious reasons was also gradually replaced with more specific social, political and institutional forms of censorship. Some hotly debated and censored texts included Harriet Beecher Stowe's *Uncle Tom's Cabin* (1852), Mark Twain's *Huckleberry Finn* (1884), Joseph Smith's *The Book of Mormon* (1830), Karl Marx and Friedrich Engels' *The Communist Manifesto* (1848) and Charles Darwin's *The Origin of the Species* (1859).

Obscenity was another common reason for censorship in the late eighteenth and early nineteenth centuries. In England, the *Proclamation for the Discouragement of Vice* by George II in 1782, the *Vagrancy Act of 1824* and the *Obscene Publications Act of 1857* censored the sale of obscene books and legally authorised their destruction. In the United States, the *Comstock Act of 1873* was accepted as a federal law that prohibited sending obscene materials through postal services. In the 1880s morality groups and vice societies such as the *New York Society for the Suppression of Vice* censored books such as Stanislaw Przybyszewski's *Homo Sapiens*, Theodore Dreiser's *The Genius* and even James Joyce's *Ulysses* (from 1922 to 1933). In the German states, censorship officially ended in 1848. *The Imperial Press Law of 1874* invalidated the government licencing of the press and prior censorship, and instead it increased the post-publication censorship of published materials. Between 1871 and 1918, the German government censored literary works based on religious, political, social and moral norms because "the empire was controlled by a narrow, premodern, antiliberal, reactionary elite of agrarian-military aristocrats and arch conservative industrialists who protected their domination by coercing opponents, manipulating political life and public opinion, and successfully blocking all progressive elements" (Stark xvi).

Besides censored books, censorship practices over press publications were expanded with the multiplication of published newspapers around the world from the seventeenth century. The growth of newspapers in Europe dates back to 1609, with the first regular printed newspaper titled *The Relation of Strasbourg* in Germany. With increasing public demand, newspapers appeared in Switzerland in 1610, in England in 1621, in France in 1631, in Denmark in 1634 and in Sweden in 1645. The growth of circulation of information simultaneously endangered the safety of nation states and empires in times of wars or civil crisis. In England, the *Licencing Act of 1662* was in place until after the Great Plague of 1664–65, and in Germany the press was heavily censored during the Thirty Years' War (1618–1648). In 1644 in England, John Milton gave a speech (entitled "Areopagitica") in Parliament on the censorship of the press and free expression; he strongly opposed the *Licencing Act of 1643*. His speech had some impact on the *Licencing Act of 1694*.

In 1766, Sweden abolished censorship and guaranteed the freedom of the press, a move that was followed by Denmark-Norway in 1770. In the

United States, the *First Amendment of the Constitution* (1787) and the *National Assembly of France* (1789) guaranteed freedom of speech and the press. In France, the *Law on the Freedom of the Press* was accepted on 29 July 1881 by the French Third Republic, confirming the freedom of the press and the right to free printing and publication. Nevertheless, practices of repressive prohibition continued in different forms and fluctuating degrees throughout the eighteenth and nineteenth centuries.[3] Censorship of colonial countries such as the UK and Russia over colonised lands such as the Baltic, Australia, Canada, India and Africa continued until the end of the nineteenth century. Censorship was abolished in Australia in 1823, while the freedom of the press was guaranteed in South Africa in 1828. The Russian Empire had a long history of strict censorship of the press until the period of 1855–1865. Between 1866 and 1905 censorship was then practiced again until its abolishment in 1917. With the increasing number of censorship practices around the world, the definition and study of censorship has become a fundamental and critical issue in literary scholarship.

From a theorical perspective, the study of censorship is defined as "an interdisciplinary field where political, legal, religious and literary histories intersect with those of the book trade, libraries, the press, theatre and

---

3 Before the 1870s, German states had strict censorship over the press and freedom of expression, and a government licence was required for the publication of books and newspapers. In the German Empire (1871–1918), the *Imperial Press Law of 1874* diminished earlier prior censorship practices, yet required the notification of printed materials and prosecution if the content was found inappropriate. Theatres, cabarets and music halls were still subject to the state licencing system. In nineteenth-century Italy, on the other hand, censorship practices (on visual arts, for instance) date back to 1861, with the unification of nation and conflicts between papacy and anti-clericalists, as well as the state and the church in the period. In eighteenth century-Russia, the emperor held the full control over censorship, however, towards the end of the period it was transferred to the Synod, the Senate and the Academy of Sciences. In early nineteenth century, the Ministry of Education (and later the Ministry of Internal Affairs) took the charge of censorship in 1804 and all public books and essays were examined by the official censor before their publication. The Bureau of Censorship also monitored authors and supervised all printed material and manuscripts for approval or refusal. (See Negri and Sironi 191–219).

film" (Stark xix).[4] Conventionally, the study of censorship concentrates on censorship policies and practices in specific countries, regimes and time periods, on certain authors and their publications, or on specific ideas. It reflects focused interests and concerns at any given cultural or historical moment and this condition prevents a ubiquitous definition of the term (Clegg, "Censorship"). It is further described as "an institutionalised, usually sanctioned form of social control involving systematic state examination and judgement of expressions intended for public dissemination" (Stark xx). Discrete actions and "repressive interventions" refer to those "formal, overt, and conscious attempts to control the public expression of opinions" (xx). There are two main types of conventional censorship practices: preventive (or prior) censorship and punitive (repressive or *ex post facto*) censorship. In preventive censorship, state authorities inspect materials before they are published and either approve or prohibit their publication. This is a strict application since expressions of thought are not made available to the public without official sanction. In punitive censorship, literary or artistic productions are controlled after their public dissemination and later they are either prohibited, destroyed, or altered by the control mechanisms. Sometimes the responsible author or publisher is even punished. This, however, is "a more permissive form of censorship" compared to preventive censorship (xx). In contemporary definitions of censorship, there are both "soft" and "hard" forms of regulation and application (Burt 18). Judith Butler contends that "explicit and implicit forms exist on a continuum in which the middle region consists of forms of censorship that are not rigo[u]rously distinguishable in this way" (249–50). For Helen Freshwater too, censorship can be viewed as "a continuum, with the brutal extremes of incarceration and murder at one end and the constitutive operation of self-censorship at the other" (11).

Since the 1960s, the study of censorship has transformed as a concept and an institution due to increasing interest in communication studies, theories of the press and the evolution of the public domain. Traditionally,

---

4 In nineteenth-century France, and in the rest of Europe, theatre was very popular and significant but the stage/theatre censorship was prevalent, too, for the state considered some theatre plays as a threat against established political, legal or social-class order (See Goldstein 240–65).

censorship is considered as "explicit acts of 'repressive intervention'" by specific institutions and authorities "to silence a subject" (Stark xix). However, contemporary interpretations suggest that censorship is "an ongoing process or system of power relationships" that is "omnipresent and inescapable, an inherent structural necessity" because all kinds of expressive acts are restricted by "underlying psychic and social forces, internalised perceptions and inhibitions", various methods of domination and exclusionary practices (xix). More broadly, the study of censorship is defined in *Censorship: A World Encyclopaedia* (2001) as any process "formal and informal, overt and overt, conscious and unconscious, by which restrictions are imposed on the collection, display, dissemination, and exchange of information, opinions, ideas and imaginative expression." (qtd in Stark xix). This, however, complicates agreement on the definition of censorship since its meaning ranges from any attempt to "control communication between people [Berger]", any actions that "limi[t] what we can read, hear or know [Jansen]" and "any 'discourse control' or 'use of semantic domination'" (qtd in Stark xix-xx).

Contemporary studies of censorship emphasise the paradoxical capacity of censorship as a form of cultural regulation that can produce as well as suppress meaning (Moore, "Censorship"). Restrictions and prohibitions shape literary works, while literature explores and pushes the limits of censorship. In the current *Oxford Dictionary of Media and Communication*, censorship is defined as "any regime or context in which the content of what is publicly expressed, exhibited, published, broadcast, or otherwise distributed is regulated or in which the circulation of information is controlled", "a regulatory system for vetting, editing, and prohibiting particular forms of public expression" and, even more generally, "the practice and process of suppression or any particular instance of this" (qtd in Moore, "Censorship"). In media studies, the censored object is information and often public access to the "the truth" is denied. In the literary field, artistic outcome is valued, however, the production and distribution of literary works are strongly controlled in accordance with common cultural values and political ideologies of the state or dominant groups. For this reason, even if they possess artistic value, literary works that contain obscene elements are frequently censored by the state, either before or after publication.

4.3.1 The Censor Within: Self-Censorship

> *Consciously or unconsciously, people censor*
> *themselves – they don't need to be called into line.*
> *(Pierre Bourdieu, "On Television")*

Although there is not a commonly agreed contemporary definition of censorship as a term, most definitions reflect three elements of the process: *"imposed act* (suppression or deletion), the *object* on which it is imposed (any communicative material), and *the authority* enforcing it (represented by the censor"* (Ben-Ari 133–4). When not overtly imposed by the authorities, censorship might be "imposed from within the individual, the outer and inner censor converging" (134). In the online edition of the *Cambridge Dictionary*, self-censorship is defined as "the control of what you say or do in order to avoid annoying or offending others but without being told officially that such control is necessary" ("Cambridge Dictionary"). Authors and publishers, for instance, might "internali[s]e the mechanisms of control" and their self-control or self-censorship can make explicit censorship more flexible or unnecessary (Stark xxi). In order to avoid any possible censorship over their work, many authors avoid writing about certain subjects, themes or genres, and, in this way, censorship significantly affects the artistic outcome produced for the public and its dissemination among certain groups. It shapes and constrains the language used by the author, as well as influencing what the public reads and how they interpret a literary work.

In many countries around the world, state censorship has been carried out as a way of controlling and defending common social, political, religious or social norms and values. However, in periods of major and rapid social and economic transformation, countries undergo a period of conflict between preserving established norms and the need for norm evolution or modernisation. Censors and writers are part of this ongoing process, yet the censors' suppression of expressions that promote or encourage social change in fact prevent the long-term stability and adaptation of society to new circumstances (Stark xxiii). Nonetheless, from an ideological point of view, censorship is a method used by politically dominant groups to preserve their interests and power by upholding their own norms and values. Stark suggests that although authorities who exercise censorship defend their repressive acts as being for the welfare of society (especially vulnerable groups such as the young, women and the less well-educated), they in fact protect the most powerful and influential members of society as well (xxiv). In *A Long Time Burning* (1969), Donald Thomas observes that censorship practices are based on fear. The institution of censorship usually aims to advocate the established order against critics, radicals and the outsiders who threaten their authority and power. That is, the practice of censorship is closely linked with power relations, struggle against authority, and the use of knowledge to increase control over society and any non-conformist ideas and expressions that might threaten the established order. In nineteenth-century Europe, for instance, different types and degrees of censorship were engaged by the elite groups and dominant classes as a method of preserving and maintaining their power and interests.

Voluntary or self-imposed censorship is more likely to occur in domains "where formal censorship is not strictly enforced" (Ben-Ari 132). Besides formal censorship practices, there are some cases in which "the borderline between formal censorship and self-censorship seems blurred" (132). Some artistic or literary works reveal the intricate and profound roots of self-imposed censorship mechanisms and the "reduced need for formal censorship when subordinate groups or individuals", such as authors and journalists, "feel that working *with* the consensus is more beneficial than working against it" (132). In most cases, when self-censorship is not applied, corrective measures are enacted on the products. To illustrate, during the reign of Abdulhamid II in the Ottoman Empire, most authors were aware that unless they practiced a form of self-censorship, they would be persecuted by the state authorities. For this reason, authors needed to have a complete understanding of "the censor's views of what can be considered objectionable, harmful, sensitive, or inconvenient" to the state policies or the public demands (134–5). Being familiar with the existent control mechanisms and punishments in formal censorship, authors exercised self-censorship that functioned as "an agent in the unconscious that is responsible for censorship" (135). The origins of the constraints that motivated intellectual artists (cultural, political, ideological, historical, religious, economic, aesthetic and psychological etc.) in the choices they made are difficult to interpret; however, formal censorship regulations of the time might provide a beneficial starting point for understanding their artistic outcome. Nonetheless, one question remains at this point regarding the ambiguous influence of (self-)censorship on artistic creation and productivity, as elaborated in the next section.

4.4 Creativity, Literature and Censorship

Creativity as a term is widely used in many disciplines to refer to scientific and artistic productions. The contemporary notion of creativity is essentially distinguished from other concepts, such as productivity, originality, inspiration, imagination, genius and intuition. Creativity as a concept has also undergone major transformations throughout history. For centuries, the term was predominantly being used in reference to a "divine, archaic" power (such as God as a creator) or as a source of inspiration for artistic productions. In the early modern period creativity referred to "special artistic" qualities (the creative artist) and later the focus shifted to the creativity of humanity and secular notions (Pope and Swann 3). Inspiration was often interpreted as a divine power transferred to the artist and it referred to an energy or stimulation in ancient history. Another term that has experienced a shift in meaning is "originality", which was initially used to refer to the "ancient, traditional" and later came to refer to things that were "novel", "innovative" and "never-have-been-done-before" from the late eighteenth century (4). The difference between "the original [initial] painting" and "an original [innovative] painting" clarifies this distinction. Creativity is also distinguished from "productivity" in the sense that it marks originality, whilst productivity is about the quantity and quality of standard works. In this sense, being a prolific writer does not always mean that the artist makes original contributions to literature. Literary works can constitute quality and impact, yet it is arguable whether they are products of novelty (creativity) or originality.

In artistic creativity, imagination is an indispensable factor and the role of imagery is in particular related to mental imagery and spatial visualisation in the creative process. Unlike creativity, the term "genius" is often used to refer to those possessing "an exceptional talent" or "a power of imagination" (Pope and Swann 5). This term was previously used to refer to tribes and people, as well as the characteristic traits of individuals. Invention in scientific research, on the other hand, refers to creating something new, whilst discovery is described as the recognition or exploration of something that already exists. If creativity is not considered an exceptional talent for invention/discovery, as in genius, is it a skill or a combination of skills? From what source does creativity emerge? In *Fiction, Intuition and Creativity* (2003), Angela Hague focuses on intuition in fictional writing and investigates whether it is a source of creativity or not. Intuition is generally defined as "a spontaneous gush coming from within, an immediate knowledge that does not derive from a rational process or logical thinking" (Samier 1). Examining a number of novelists' (the Bröntes, James, Woolf and Lessing) expressions about their own creative process, Hague argues that creative intuition is "a state of mind [or consciousness] that is necessary for creative activity to flourish" and it determines the content or structure of a literary work (5). Intuition also functions as "a mode of perception" and "obsessive consciousness" and sometimes it helps the author to be "a scrutini[s]er of his/her own creative processes" (8). This self-consciousness, however, often demands a suitable psychic environment for "introspection of feelings" that frequently emerge "during very relaxed, near sleep-like states" (qtd in Hauge 5).

In an article in *The Psychology of Creative Writing* (2009), Jane Piirto focuses on the personalities of creative writers and whether they have any core/common personality traits. In this seminal work, the researcher divides writers into two main categories: the ones "writing from the ivory tower" and those in "the field of battle" (Piirto 3). Some of shared qualities of creative adults are found to be "creativity, imagination, insight, intuition, introversion, naiveté, openness to experience [...] overexcitability, motivation or passion for work, perceptiveness, persistence, preference for complexity, resilience, risk-taking, self-discipline, self-efficacy, tolerance for ambiguity, volition, or will" (3–4). In psychopathology, creative writers are sometimes described as "markedly deviant" from the public and it is noted that they have some tendencies to have affective disorders or to be "depressive, schizoid, hysterical or psychopathic" (12). Writers are considered as "both sicker and healthier psychologically than people in general... The face they turn to the world is sometimes one of pain, often of protest, something of distance and withdrawal, and certainly they are emotional" (qtd in Piirto 12). Moreover, their intense sensitivity often alters the way they perceive themselves and apprehend the outside world. In addition to these qualities, some creative artists are heavily influenced by the effects of ambition, envy, or desire for fame, which might damage their friendships with other writers. Rejections from publishers might contribute to stress or anxiety combined with ambition. A dependent or patronised writer might recognise others' demands or expectations and accept their control/ pressure over their work in order to conform to social and cultural codes simply to satisfy economic concerns or to achieve fame.

A significant motive for creative writers is the need to make sense of the world they are living in and their inner world, to live with a purpose (Storr 87). The actualisation of these types of goals largely depends on some personality traits, such as autonomy, independence, persistence, non-conformity, motivation, subjectivity and confidence, accompanied by the delights of creative endeavour. This creative process is also influenced by the artist's other features, such as deviance, impulsiveness, playfulness, daydreaming, anxiety, changing affect/mood, which can simultaneously contribute to and complicate creative performance. Although creative authors are more likely to be divided within themselves and some experience mental illnesses or have eccentricities, they can help others become aware of some aspects of their own world with their perceptive and sensitive outlook. In creative activity, however, not only the personality traits of the artists but also their past experiences and individual skills, influence the final production. In a study carried out by Hennessey and Amabile on the conditions of creativity, it is found that intrinsic motivation is highly affected by social and environmental factors and it can have a consistently negative or positive impact on the creative performance of the artist (11–43). In "The Soul of Man under Socialism" (1891), Oscar Wilde contends that the creativity of the individual can only flourish in times of leisure. The production of ancient Greek philosophy is also often associated with their wealth and comfort since their slaves did all the manual work, which left the philosophers with sufficient time to engage in creative activities. This aspect adds economic relief as a facilitator in providing the necessary conditions and environment for creative activity, rather than regarding it as an indispensable prerequisite.

Linking creative performance and productions with censorship is a beneficial approach since they are intimately interrelated and have a paradoxical and ambiguous impact on each other. There are a number of questions to be asked along this line, including: is censorship always a threat to/a negative factor for creativity? Do creative actions need limits or boundaries to push against? Were the best literary works written in periods of censorship or oppression? Is self-censorship an individual choice based on voluntary action or fear? Are the best artists always non-conformists? Despite the obvious distinctions between generations and periods in human history, censorship has always existed in some form, with changing rules, values and boundaries. The freedom of the artist has often been restricted by certain boundaries for various reasons, such as social safety, protection of cultural and religious values, or political ideologies. On one level, limitations mark the point where the artistic creation will begin/flourish. On another level, they prevent the transmission of the artist's message to the public. The double-edged nature of censorship in this sense can both protect and harm others/the artist when it is misused. In order to make an original contribution to literature, the creative writer should have knowledge of what has been published before. Yet, originality and creative expression might not be achieved or reach the readership if literary censorship only allows for the publication and dissemination of standard texts.

Paradoxically, censorship makes the freedom of creative expression more meaningful and valuable since transgression is meaningless without limits. Recent historical and theoretical studies on the concept of censorship and its practices have led to new questions and approaches to its ambiguous influence on authors and literary creativity: does conforming to restrictive norms or censorship enhance/trigger creativity or hinder artistic production in any way? Diverging from the common belief that censorship limits or distorts literary production or creativity to a great extent, in *Censorship and the Limits of the Literary* (2015), Nicole Moore suggests that literature and censorship are producing each other, and they are "mutually constitutive" (1–8). The productive power of censorship is also acknowledged by Judith Butler, who notes in *Excitable Speech* (1997) that "it is not only privative but formative as well" (n. p.). In this sense, censorship is interpreted as "the secret sharer" of artistic production since it can foster creativity and drive literary production (Heiler 49). Some authors use a strategy that allows them to transgress taboos or prohibitions and successfully camouflage "the subversive and the repugnant", that is, the "politically undesirable" (50). Elusive, opaque or multi-dimensional literary works (texts and discourses) create space for "subversive impulses that may not be easily identified" (50). Under strict censorship practices, creativity can still flourish and thrive, yet only to a certain extent. In this respect, the existence of original literary contributions cannot be directly or solely linked to oppressive periods. A certain level of independence and tolerance is always necessary for the transmission of original and creative works to the public readership.

The significance of literature in working against dogmatic thinking is highlighted by Milan Kundera as follows: "Ideology wants to convince you that its truth is absolute. A novel shows you that everything is relative" (7). The double-edged function of fictional works creates not only an escape from the monotonous routine of everyday life but also shows the reader "the possibilities of freedom" and a different life (Albin n.p). Literature encourages the exploration of new alternatives and possibilities through distinctive and controversial perspectives. Literary works that do not conform to traditional structures or norms foreground the possibility of change by their very form (O'Learly et.al. 15). Catherine O'Learly claims that "wherever censorship exists so too do imaginative efforts to evade and subvert it" (20). These creative consequences of censorship restrictions involve explicit negotiations with censors, the use of symbolism and other techniques to disguise or veil a political message and get the work published. Furthermore, as Dallimore notes, banning a book can even increase its visibility and validity and "guarantee its place in cultural history" (95). For Butler, "the regulation that *states what it does not want stated* thwarts its own desire", bringing with it an attention and desire to speak the unspeakable (131–2).

In self-censorship, many artists tailor their creative productions according to their readership or publishers' demands but this action deteriorates their original work (Doyle, "Self-censorship is the Enemy of Creativity"). This practice occurs in two main ways: textual censorship through cuts, omissions or revisions, and the writer's alteration of his/her own image by using a pseudonym or changing the date of birth or background information (Ducas 111). For the artist who practices art with sincerity and is faithful to his/her ideals, conforming to general opinion is a kind of death. Financial concerns driven by the risk of displeasing or offending the readership, or other external forms of social, religious or political pressure, curtail self-expression and push artists to self-censor. Nevertheless, as noted above, some non-conformist artists use "creative ways to circumvent the problem", although this approach "stunts the possibility of the artist's creative development from its very wellspring" (Doyle, "Self-censorship is the Enemy of Creativity"). Prior to the publication of literary works, publishers, editors and translators also make some voluntary/involuntary interventions or textual cuts before the final submission of the book to state authorities and the public readership (Bourdieu 138). In this way, they play the role of censor, either consciously or unconsciously, by engaging their internalised social and cultural norms of the period. In fact, these forms of censorship practices are the most effective and the least noticeable ones in the literary market. In *Censorship and Silencing* (1998), Robert C. Post addresses discursive practices maintained by censorship in society and notes that if they prevail in social life and are internalised, they will become "the norm rather than the exception" (Post 2). Therefore, "at its most successful, censorship is internalised and self-censorship is practised, consciously or unconsciously" in society (O'Learly et. al. 19).

These types of implicit or explicit forms of censorship practices inevitably influence the artistic outcome since the artist either diverts from his/her original intention and alters his/her final product, or the original work is altered by publishers, editors or translators to some extent, which distorts its essence, original content, structure and form. Institutionalised censorship practices impose intentional or compulsory avoidance of certain subjects, genres or plots in literary works. In this regard, whilst acknowledging creative efforts and outcomes triggered by the relationship between literature and censorship by intellectual artists, this study contends that the destructive and restrictive power of censorship over literary production outweighs its smaller-scale creative impact on authorship and creative productions in literary history. Artistic freedom provides more opportunities for original and creative contributions with new approaches, perspectives, literary forms and styles. Formulations and motivations of artistic creation will be elaborated in the third chapter of this book through the analysis of novels. Before moving to that section, some background information is presented on the distinctive conditions of the publishing world, authorship, and censorship practices in England, Norway and the Ottoman Empire in the nineteenth century.

5. Literary Publishing and Censorship in England, Norway and the Ottoman Empire

5.1 Victorian Publishing and Literary Censorship

In nineteenth-century England, there was a dramatic increase in the publication of novels, periodicals and newspapers, as well as in the population of reading public, after the emergence and advance of the printing press technologies in Europe. The increasing number of publications and demand of the readership and publishers resulted in a corresponding emergence of writers and journalists as a new professional class in the literary circles of Victorian London. Professional authors, however, had to support themselves with insufficient wages through financial contracts signed with editors and publishing companies (Severn 169). In the period, the dominant and most popular form of publication for fiction in the UK was initially the "three-decker" or "three-volume" novel, a publishing system that increased the cost of books for the readers and hindered their sale to circulating libraries and subscriptions (Goode xiv). Since the income was not sufficient either, some authors had to sell the copyright to their works and thus they could not benefit from the sale of new editions. Serialisation of short stories or chapters of novels within periodicals, or publication of a cheaper one-volume novel after the initial book publication were among several alternatives used by authors to provide financial relief.

Gissing, for instance, sold the copyright to *Demos* (1886) and *New Grub Street* (1891) due to financial concerns. Although *New Grub Street* had originally been written and published as a three-decker novel, it was later revised and published as a one-volume novel upon the publisher's request. In the Victorian publishing industry, there were two distinct types of book production depending on their economic or aesthetic value: the first included valuable and qualified works and the second included commercial best-seller books, purchased at a lower price and consumed by the reading public in their leisure time and as family reading. Towards the end of the century, the Victorian publishing industry underwent a major transformation with the advent of the *Net Book Agreement* in the 1890s, which increased the popularity of serial fiction and one-volume novels and led to major shifts in the readership and publishers' demands in England (Feltes 4).

The readership in the Victorian era often benefited from circulating libraries and subscriptions as a way to access literary works (three-decker novels in particular) that they could not afford to purchase. Subscribers of a circulating library could withdraw a number of books at a time after paying an annual fee (Arata 40). For publishers, selling their books in bulk was profitable and they could more easily predict their revenue, which gave them the opportunity to publish books by new or less well-known authors. Being in the "select list" of the Mudie's library (the most popular library at the time) could advance the popularity of an author and his/her book (40). However, circulating libraries could at the same time hinder or restrict innovation in literature as they rejected works that they claimed would not suit the literary tastes of the public. In late-Victorian London, £100 annual income per year was "a bare minimum" for supporting one's family and £150 was identified as the "line separating the middle from the working classes, since incomes below that level were exempt from taxes" (qtd in Arata 43). In the 1880s, 65 % of the total reported annual income was between £150 and £300. In Gissing's *New Grub Street*, to illustrate, Harold Biffen expects at least £15 for *Mr Bailey, Grocer* and half-profits for its future editions; Reardon, on the other hand, receives no money from his first novel, whilst his second novel brings him £25. His third novel is sold for £50, *On Neutral Ground* for £100, *Hubert Reed* for £100, and *Margaret Home* for £75. At this point, Reardon's financial failure as an impoverished author is "put into unmistakable figures" (qtd in Arata 42). That is, the income both Biffen and Reardon earn from the publication of their novels remains much lower than that of a middle-class person of the period. The two writers are in need of an additional job, such as working as a tutor or occasionally writing stories, reviews or essays, to provide some financial relief. Their annual income is far from providing them with the comfortable life of a middle-class member in late-Victorian London.

The phenomenon of the serial format as monthly instalments of novels in the UK dates back to 1817 (shortly after the emergence of the three-volume

format in 1815) with *Blackwood's Monthly Magazine* (Brake 3–4). Most
of the instalments were later published as a one-volume book. Since the
price of most three-decker novels was too high for the public, authors
writing for serials aimed to reach a wider audience and the readers could
access their works at a cheaper cost than that of circulating libraries or
booksellers from 1830 onwards. The long presence of Sundays, weeklies,
monthlies, annuals and dailies, such as the *Edinburgh*, the *Westminster*,
the *Athenaeum*, the *Spectator, Punch, The Times*, the *Examiner* and the
Penny Magazine, in the literary market demonstrates their cultural role
and intellectual power for the readership. The number of serials increased
continuously between 1800 and 1900, with an ever-wider range and acces-
sibility to the reading public. After 1848, single-volume reprints of serials
and cheap editions of railway stories and novels adopted a significant place
in the market. Whilst in the early decades of the century weekly serials
appealed more to the ordinary reader and monthly instalments were considered more respectable forms, from the 1860s, new works by respectable
authors began to be read by middle-class readers as well (Law 73). Charles
Dickens' *The Pickwick Papers* (1836–37) and *Oliver Twist* (1837–39), for
instance, initially appeared in monthly magazines such as *Chapman and
Hall* and *Bentley's Miscellany*.

Gissing himself was aware of the financial potential of the serial publication and his novel *A Life's Morning* (1888) was published in instalments
in the *Cornhill*. He earned about £50 from this, including selling the rights
of the book format to Smith, Elder (Law 74). In a letter written to his sister
Ellen in 1888, Gissing admitted that this format was "as a rule twice as
profitable as the vol. form" (Mattheisen et. al. 172). However, compared
to his works published in one- or three-volume books by publishers, his
number of published serials remained relatively low. Most of Gissing's earlier short stories were published "either unsigned or under a pseudonym,
in American journals during his years of exile from 1876" and there was
a small number of his fictional publications in the London press until
1892 (Law 71). By 1893, the number of his literary works published in
instalments had reached about 80, including his short stories and sketches,
and *Eve's Ransom* (1895) in the *Illustrated London News*. Compared
to other short story writers earning their living through serial fiction,
Gissing's contributions were less visible in the literary market. Possibly

for this reason, Walter Besant stated in the January 1895 issue of *The Author* that he had hardly been aware of Gissing's contributions in the serials before:

> In an advertisement of a new periodical, "the Minister", one observes with some surprise the name of Mr. George Gissing as the contributor of a story [The Salt of the Earth]. With surprise, not because he ought not to be there but because this powerful writer has never before, so far as I know, appeared in a serial. I hear now of other magazines which have at last found him out. I have never been able to understand the comparative silence with which the very fine work of this writer has been received. It is, perhaps, because his themes have been gloomy [...] (qtd in Law 71)

In fact, Gissing had published at least 38 short stories in periodicals before, yet Besant was probably unaware of that because most of Gissing's contributions were published in America and some of them were either unsigned or written under a pseudonym. Gissing's main interest remained in writing novels unless he was in need of extra income, which pushed him to write short stories and essays. His stories boasted literary value and well-structured plots, yet his novels were more widely welcomed and known by the reading public.

Victorian publishing was profoundly influenced by the demands of the public and the circulating libraries, and although there was no explicit censorship legislations or regulations regarding literary production, authors and their works were under the influence of the changing conditions of the literary market and readership. Censorship in Victorian literature was practiced mainly through "informal, non-legal means, such as [...] the long-standing monopoly of circulating libraries such as Mudie's Select Library and W.H. Smith's" (Deal 9). Due to the increasing popularity of the three-decker novel form in England from the 1830s, the readers mainly depended upon borrowing these books from circulating libraries (Griest 78–9). As the largest circulating library in the country, Mudie's practiced a certain power and control over newly published works and their circulation, and it had an intimate relationship with publishers as well. Mudie's further applied strict moral standards and avoided purchasing any books that could be considered inappropriate for family reading; it would remove any work that received complaints from readers from its shelves. Èmile Zola's *A Modern Lover*, a one-volume novel translated into English, was removed from the Mudie's library for its "immorality", and as a response to this censorship George Moore wrote an essay entitled "Literature at Nurse" and campaigned against not only circulating libraries but also the three-decker novel form (Deal 10).

About a decade later, the literary market underwent a dramatic transformation and a transition from the three-volume novel form to a one-volume form took place in England (Deal 10). The statistics on published works also confirm this change: whereas in 1894, a total of 184 three-volume novels were published by British publishers, this number was only 4 by 1897, which reflects the demise of the former format (Griest 208). A number of essential changes in the literary marketplace, such as the re-sale of used copies of three-decker novels by circulating libraries, cheap reprints of new books by publishers, and the prevalence of free public libraries, played a significant role in this fading interest in the old format. This new form of one-volume novel provided some degree of artistic freedom for authors and also shortened the time allocated to publishing and reading literary works (Deal 11). In the following decades, Mudie's library circulated one-volume novels with fewer restrictions over new/innovative fictional works in the market.

Victorian censorship was more effective on pornographic works with the introduction of *The Obscene Publications Act of 1857*. There were also a number of anti-vice societies, such as the *National Vigilance Association*, a pressure group that worked on "urging to the police to take action against sellers of pornography, petitioning parliament for improved obscenity legislation, and occasionally initiating private prosecutions against objectionable works" (Deal 11). In *A Long Time Burning* (1969), Donald Thomas observes that censorship practices were more threatening by the end of the century due to the "risk of legal prosecution" in England (262–3). That is, unconventional literary works were less likely to be released by the publishers in the restrictive legal atmosphere (Deal 12). To illustrate, in early twentieth century, D.H. Lawrence's *The Rainbow* and Radclyffe Hall's *Well of Loneliness* were banned in 1915 and in 1928 respectively as a result of an obscenity prosecution.

In *On Liberty* (1859), John Stuart Mill drew attention to the prevalent effect of social pressure and censorship in England as follows: "[In] our times, from the highest class of society to the lowest, every one lives under the eye of a hostile and dreaded censorship" (264). In this statement, Mill emphasises public opinion/censure rather than formal censorship practices conducted by official institutions. In fact, this condition refers to "multifarious and not easily identifiable ways" of censorship as "less overt forms of regulation, such as the economic constraints of the marketplace, and more dispersed forms of influence" in nineteenth-century England (Wong 1–2). These forms of implicit control and regulations restrict the content and form of specific contexts in the literary field and other areas in art. Public opinion can be described as a form of subtle but forbidding control that is more easily embedded in people's lives and has a profound impact on their final choices. This creates a kind of social censorship that naturalises the "invalidat[ion of] any opposition" and avoids rational thought in favour of feelings as "determinant of behaviour" (qtd in Wong 16).

The power of public taste and demand over artistic expression is further defined as a "social tyranny" by Mill (220). Censorship, the literary market and public demand are considered as constraints on the "autonomy of art" and the artist (Wong 14). Popular public taste and social moralities set artificial boundaries for artistic and intellectual production in the period. The reading public was defined by Henry James as "millions for whom taste is but an obscure, confused, immediate instinct" and social control was condemned by George Moore as "the tittle-tatty of the nursery and the lady's drawing room" (qtd in Wong 14). The public's opinion and publishers' demands, therefore, were considered a type of "debilitating censorship" and this led to anxiety among some authors since they could function as a form of control that "determin[ed] the financial viability of publication" and artistic production (15–6). Gissing also criticises the public censorship of sexuality in English novels in his book *Charles Dickens: A Critical Study* (1898), as follows:

> The Emperor Augustus, we are told, objected to the presence of women at the public games when athletes appeared unclad; but he saw nothing improper in their watching the death combats of gladiators. May we not find a parallel to this in *the English censorship*? To exhibit the actual course of things in a story of lawless (nay, or of lawful) *love is utterly forbidden*; on the other hand, *a novelist may indulge in ghastly bloodshed to any extent of which his stomach is capable*. Dickens, the great writer, even appears on a public platform and recites with terrible power the murder of a prostitute by a burglar, yet hardly a voice

is raised in protest. Gore is perfectly decent; but the secrets of an impassioned
heart are too shameful to come before us even in a whisper. (205–6)

The acceptability of descriptions of extreme violence and the rejection
of love or sexuality in English fiction are criticised by Gissing and he
emphasises the incoherence between the public's attitude and demands in
this passage. The example of the gladiators in the Roman Empire and also
that from Dickens' novels draws our attention to the historical background
and continuity of censorship practices in specific historical periods and the
contradiction between embracing, watching or reading about violent acts,
whilst recoiling from love and affection in both life and fiction. At this
point, Gissing criticises the discrepancy between the application of realism
and realistic representations of the natural course of living in history and
English literature.

5.2 Literary Production and Censorship in Nordic Countries

Since the socio-economic and historical conditions of Norway, as one of
the Nordic countries (Denmark, Sweden, Iceland and Finland), were dramatically different from those of the UK in the late nineteenth century, its
economic, demographic and literary history also took a different route.
For about three centuries, Norway had been influenced by Danish politics, literature and culture; however, after its independence in 1814, the
country began to witness gradual yet promising progress in every field.
After independence, Norway experienced one of the highest rates of population growth in Europe. Due to the decrease in the death rate and a
stable increase in the birth rate from 1800 to 1900, the country's population nearly tripled and increased from about 800,000 in the early part
of the decade to 2,240,000 in 1900 (Lieberman 52). These demographic
changes took place in pre-industrial Norway and by 1900 the population
in rural areas constituted 72 % of the total population since it was an
agrarian country. Norway's economic growth in the period was essentially
based on an industrial revolution and "self-sustaining economic-growth
mechanisms", which enabled "the nation [to] bec[o]me integrated into the
developed part of the world economy" as a developing country (Sejersted
40). Norway's involvement in foreign markets, its exportation of fish and
timber, shipping and shipbuilding enabled an export-led economic growth

from the 1840s onwards. From the 1870s, exports of wood processing, textile, chemicals and metals grew continuously until 1895. The state's political and social strategies for the modernisation of the nation and growing industries transformed Norway into a developed European country in the following decades.

Norway began to use the printing press in 1643, "almost two centuries after it had been introduced in the rest of Europe, hindering the development of the territory's intellectual life" until the nineteenth century (Petersen 1738). In 1689, the dual monarchy of Norway and Denmark was transformed into "an absolutist kingdom" (1739). Enlightenment opinions had a gradual impact in Norway through Norwegian writers who lived in Denmark and published their works in Danish, such as Ludvig Holberg (1684–1754). In 1772, the Danish language was accepted as the official language of the two countries and students were taught Danish history at Norwegian grammar schools. After the French Revolution in 1789, political discussions among intellectuals in the *Det Norske Selskab* (The Norwegian Society, established in 1772) and the abolition of censorship in Norway and Denmark in 1770 led to an increase in the number of periodicals published in Copenhagen, Bergen and Trondheim. A number of articles in *Hermoder* (published in Denmark) drew attention to the significance of society "in shaping the desire for Norwegian independence" and carried implications for a more independent political state for Norway. After Norway's independence from Denmark in 1814, Sweden took control of the country from 1815 to 1905. The union with Sweden was unlike its relationship with Denmark since Norway continued to use its constitution liberally during that period.

Literary culture in Norway revived with mass production and the increasing number of literary works published after its independence from Denmark (Rossi 421). In this period, significant progress was made in the fields of music and literature, with the works of Bjørnstjerne Bjørnson, Henrik Ibsen and Edvard Munch (Naess xiv). By the late 1860s, Norwegian (national) literature was essentially romantic and constituted the dominant forms, such as poems, folk tales and history books. From the 1870s, however, *Det Moderne Gennembrud* (Modern Breakthrough), a literary movement encouraged by the Danish critic Georg Brandes, marked a sudden and clean break in literary history, with romanticism being replaced with realism (Downs 10–1). In the 1890s, Norwegian literature progressed with the innovative works of poets, playwrights and writers such as Arne Garborg (1851–1924), Knut Hamsun (1859–1952) and Hans Kink (1865–1926), intellectual artists who were "concerned with the evocation of moods, reveries, and the soul life of the individual" (11). Unlike in the UK where the standard language in publications was English, well-known Norwegian writers of the Modern Breakthrough – Ibsen, Bjørnson, Kielland and Lie – were writing their works in Danish rather than in *Landsmall* (country language, *Nynorsk*) since they defended a Dano-Norwegian continuum. Also, the three-volume format was not popular in the way it was in England, and the number of trilogies was limited to only a few examples before the interwar period. After Norway's independence in the early nineteenth century, Copenhagen continued to be a cultural and literary centre for Norway and Denmark, and a Danish publishing company called Gyldendal continued to publish literary works by Norwegian writers (Ferguson 33).

An "institutionali[s]ed prior censorship" was established in Sweden in 1766 with "limited abolition of censorship" and in Denmark-Norway in 1770 with the "complete abolition of censorship" (Laursen 100). Prior censorship was practiced in Sweden and Denmark-Norway from the early decades of the eighteenth century until it was entirely banned through constitutional laws by the mid-century.[5] In particular, with the constitutions of 1809, 1814 and 1849, freedom of the press was declared, and any types of censorship practices were prohibited. Nevertheless, complete liberty was not given "since libel, slander, blasphemy, and obscenity were still punishable" and public opinion had a profound impact on censorship practices (100). The main objectives of these practices were either preserving authority and power, or protecting the public against threatening moral, political, religious or obscene ideas and materials. Whilst in the

---

5 In 1686 in Finland, the *Office of Book Censorship* was in charge of monitoring imported/published literary works and publishers needed to get an approval/license for their books. In the nineteenth century, with a law in 1829 (until 1865), censorship practices increased in Finland, especially on the press publications and some newspapers were not allowed to continue publication (See Laursen 100–121).

early decades of the nineteenth century, prior censorship was used to control communication, by the end of the period the public was given the right to bring charges for obscenity and blasphemy. These changes regarding censorship laws and nature were intimately linked to the advances taking place in technology, transformation of social structures, and the increase in the number of newspapers and pamphlets, printing machines, authors and reading public.

In the Swedish Constitution, the *1766 Ordinance* confirmed that "unrestricted mutual information about useful topics will not only lead to development of the sciences and economic productivity [but] ought to be considered one of the best means for improvement of morality and obedience to the law [and] the earlier established censor's office now should be completely abolished" (qtd in Laursen 104). Prior censorship was still practiced for some religious, moral, economic and political disputes that might lead to wrong interpretations of the doctrines of Christianity, state administration and public morality, however. Between 1766 and 1769, Sweden's first daily newspaper and about 80 new periodicals were established. The number of published political pamphlets amounted to about 434 in 1769 and this number reached up to 583 by 1772. However, a majority of these publications were financially supported by the French, Russians, English and Danes. The Ordinance Law regarding censorship was abolished in 1772 under the reign of Gustavus III. Yet prior censorship was still practiced by printing houses and controls on the press were tight in the period.

In 1770, the Denmark-Norway monarchy declared unlimited liberty of the press, although this was later narrowed down with police control over the press and published materials in 1773 (Laursen 105). This new law was widely publicised in the press and journals both at the national and international level. The Danish, English, German and even American newspapers announced this news in their countries. However, as Laursen notes, the liberty of the press was not entirely enacted due to three possible reasons, as follows. The public was reluctant about expression of any radical opinions and they did not have complete faith in the applicability of the freedom of expression and the press. They believed that they would face prosecution if they published non-conformist ideas that went against religious or state authorities. Political debates and resistance acts were also not welcomed in Danish political culture (111). On 9 October 1771, a new version of the law with limitations to the liberty of the press was printed:

1) In order that the freedom to write and print granted on 14 September 1770 may not be misused to thereby transgress other civilian laws, all libel, lampoon, and rebellious publications shall in the future, as before, be subject to the established punishment.

2) Although all censorship is abolished, nevertheless every author who writes something shall be responsible that it is not contrary to existing laws and ordinances.

3) Printers cannot be allowed to print any book or publication if he [sic] does not know who the author is, as he is to be responsible if he cannot name the author, to which end no book may be printed that does not contain the author's or printer's name. (qtd in Laursen 111)

Later, in 1773, the police control over press publications was legitimised by the government without enacting prior censorship (112–3). This police power was enforced until 1790, when their rights were transferred to independent courts in the country. Several historical events, such as the French Revolution and wars in the 1790s, increased the government's control over printed materials and prior censorship was practiced, allowing some writers to be exiled. During the Napoleonic wars, censorship practices were even tighter. After a short period of peace during the first decades of the nineteenth century (there is only one recorded case from 1814–30), there were more than 220 cases on censorship practices impacting newspapers, books and pamphlets from 1831–1847. Following an increase in clashing groups and ideas, on 28 January 1848 press censorship was prohibited again and more attention was paid to obscenity and slander than religious or political issues.

The Norwegians gained their independence from Denmark through the Eidsvoll Constitution in 1814 and Article 100 stated that "an entire liberty of the press shall take place [...] It is allowed everybody freely to deliver his opinions of government or any other subject [sic]" (qtd in Laursen 114). However, in these statements there were some conditions on which citizens could be punished. Citizens would not be punished for any published materials unless they were found to be intentionally and willingly disobedient to legislations or provoking others in non-conformist acts against religious or moral values or constitutive rules. Those who resisted state laws or made false statements or accusations against others would be subject to prosecution for breaking the constitutional law. These practices mainly depended on the interpretation of published materials by authorities and the freedom of the press was restricted through possible penalties and punishments. In nineteenth-century Norway, there were two further types of censorship practices: banning the ideas and publications of Jews and expelling them from the country and applying censorship over materials that contradicted the moral standards of the public and controversial religious issues such as threatening Christian values. To illustrate, Henrik Ibsen's play *Ghosts* (1881) was banned and not performed in Norway until 1883 and Hans Jaeger's *Fra Kristiania-Boheme* (1885) was prohibited for obscenity and the writer exiled as a result of its publication.

5.3 Literature, Press and Censorship in the Ottoman Empire

The dominant literary genres in the Ottoman Empire until the nineteenth century were mainly poetry –carrying an imprint of Persian and Chagatai literatures – and prose, specifically books on history, theology, mysticism and travel. From the 1300s to the late 1800s, Ottoman poetry was the dominant literary form and it constituted a variety of forms, such as *Sufi poetry*, *gazel* and *kasîde* ("qasīdah"). Along with the transformation of the social, economic and political conditions of the Empire with the influence of European ideas and the development of printing and the press, traditional literary forms started to lose their attraction and validity for the new generation, who wanted to modernise literature and the Ottoman state. The Empire survived over six centuries (from the fourteenth century to the early twentieth century) until its fall and the establishment of the Turkish Republic in 1923. The imperial decline during the eighteenth and nineteenth centuries was followed by resistance to change, initial contact with the West (Europe), military and internal reforms until the Tanzimat era in 1839, and a series of reforms aiming at the modernisation of the Empire, in particular during the reigns of Abdulmecid I (ruled 1839–61) and Abdulaziz (ruled 1861–76).

The emergence and development of the novel genre in the Ottoman Empire dates back to the nineteenth century and is intimately linked with the multiplication of press publications and periodicals in the period. In Europe the novel genre was already well-established by the nineteenth century and the first examples of serials had appeared a hundred years before with reprinted or translated works such as Daniel Defoe's *Robinson Crusoe* and Fielding's *Joseph Andrews* (Law 6). In England, Charles Dickens' *The Pickwick Papers* was considered the first successful original serial, published in 1836. In France, serialised novels ("roman feuilleton" in French) were used to increase the circulation of periodicals in the 1830s and 1840s. The translation of novels by popular authors such as Alexander Dumas, Victor Hugo and Eugène Sue successfully increased circulation in the period (Benjamin 125). The history of the novel tradition in the Empire was thereby distinct from that of Europe since new literary genres, such as novels and plays, were introduced into the Empire through translations of Western literature as serials in periodicals and newspapers (Serdar and Tutumlu Serdar 5). After the Tanzimat reform (1839), European ideas and literature had a greater impact on intellectuals and journalists. The first play published as a serial in Ottoman-Turkish was *Şair Evlenmesi* (1860, "The Poet's Marriage") and the first serialised novel in the Empire was entitled *Taaşşuk-u Talat ve Fitnat* (1872; "The Love of Talat and Fitnat"). Since the press and literature were highly interconnected in this process, the public acquired their first knowledge of the conventions of Western novels and plays through translated works. Some of these works included Victor Hugo's *Les Misérables* (1862), translated and published in the same year in *Ruzname-i Ceride-i Havadis* (as "Mağdurun Hikâyesi" or "Sefiller"); François-René de Chateaubriand's *Atala* (1869), translated and published in *Hakayikül Vekayi*; the translation of Jacques-Henri Bernardin de Saint-Pierre's *Paul et Virginie* (1870), published in *Mümeyyiz*; and Alexandre Dumas' *Le Comte de Monte-Cristo* (1871), translated and published in *Diyojen* (Serdar and Tutumlu Serdar 5).

Of the European countries, the impact of French literature and culture on the new Ottoman literature and culture was greater than that of other countries, including Germany and England. Western culture and literature were effectively made accessible to the public through translations and teaching French as a foreign language. In the nineteenth century, about 45 % of all translated texts and 75 % of all adaptations in the Empire were based on French literature (Ayaydın Cebe 110). Of these translations, modern novels and stories constituted 85 % and the remainder included translations of plays, biographies and poems from French literary works. Translations from Arabic and Persian literature in effect followed French literature. Between 1859 and 1901 a total of 988 poems were translated in newspapers, periodicals and books and most of them (allegedly 782) were translated from French (Kolcu 659–60). One of the reasons for the prevalence of translations from French literature was expatriate journalists who had studied in France or were exiled due to the censorship practices of the Ottoman state. To illustrate, Şinasi and Ziya Paşa lived in France, England and Switzerland and Namık Kemal in England in exile; however, they continued to produce satirical works, plays and poems that criticised the Empire and favoured the modernisation process.[6] The establishment of private colleges and the Chamber of Translation (1821), as well as education in French language (following Arabic and Persian) at secondary schools are among other critical reasons for the dominance of French language and literature in the Empire (Ayaydın Cebe 60).

In the Ottoman press, the first critiques and summaries of plays were published in *Ceride-i Havadis* ("Register of News", established in 1840) and *Şair Evlenmesi* was written and published by Şinasi in the fourth issue of *Tercüman-ı Ahval* ("Interpreter of Conditions") in 1860. Translated materials continued to appear in serial form until the publication of Şemsettin Sami's *Taaşşuk-u Talat ve Fitnat* in 1872 (Serdar and Tutumlu Serdar 6). The dramatic increase in the number of circulated newspapers and periodicals after the 1860s also contributed to the abundance of serialised novels and plays in Ottoman-Turkish and other languages, such as Arabic, Persian, French and Armenian. According to a bibliographic study conducted by Hasan Duman (2000), before 1928 (with the use of the Latin alphabet) 2,526 periodicals were published

---

6 Among other forms of literature, theatre is often considered "a particular threat because of its potential for political mobilisation" (O'Learly et. al. 15). Theatre is one of the areas that allow for "the exploration of unusual perspectives and values, and speculation about alternative visions of society" (16). Since it can display or perform on stage what is untolerated elsewhere and expose repressed issues in society and workings of authorial power, it may function as an alternative to avoid censorship practices on stage.

in the Empire. Within these publications, both translated and original works played a significant role. Whilst there were only 13 translated and copyrighted novels published from 1840–1869, this number increased to 81 from 1870–1879, 290 from 1880–1889 and finally to 751 from 1890–1899 (Erkul Yagci 92). To illustrate, in the daily issues of *İkdam* (1894–1928), 302 short stories and 52 novels (either translated or original) were published (qtd in Çıkla 45). Between 1872 and 1928, 235 novels were published in book form and most of them were first serialised in newspapers (Serdar and Serdar 8). In the period between 1877 and 1900, literary works of prolific writers such as Ahmet Mithat, Halit Ziya and Hüseyin Rahmi were serialised in newspapers such as *Tercüman-ı Hakikat*, *Hizmet*, *Servet-i Fünûn* and *İkdam*. Serialisation of novels in newspapers facilitated readers' responses to the text and sometimes led to alterations and omissions based on public pressure. Censorship of serials was also strictly applied when it was deemed necessary by the authorised institutions. Hüseyin Rahmi Gürpınar's *Alafranga* ("The European") for instance, was first serialised in *İkdam* in 1901; however, it was later censored and then re-serialised as *Şıpsevdi* in 1909.

Unlike the development of the press and printed newspapers in Europe dating back to the seventeenth century, the first Ottoman newspaper *Takvim-i Vakayi* ("The Calender of Events") was published in 1831. Foreign publications such as the French Bulletin *des Nouvelles* (1795) and *La Gazette Française de Constrantinople* (1796) were part of a "French policy to promote the French revolution" in the Empire (16). This was followed by the dissemination of private French newspapers such as *Spectateur de l'Orient* and *Le Moniteur Ottoman* in the 1820s and 1830s. *Takvim-i Vakayi* was published on the order of the sultan Mahmud II to inform the public about the state's opinions after the lost war against Russia and the loss of control of Egypt (qtd in Baykal 17). The first privately-owned newspaper in the Ottoman language was *Ceride-i Havadis*, published in 1840 as a "self-official organ" funded by the state (17). As the number of privately-owned newspapers in other languages and in the Ottoman language increased, the desire to keep them under control also mounted. Prior to 1858, there was no legislation to control the press. However, based on a communiqué issued in 1849 by the Ministry of Foreign Affairs, every embassy was required to inform the Ministry before the publication of

periodicals and books (İskit 5–10). In 1857, publication licenses were provided by the Council of Education and the Ministry of Police. The first pre-
cautionary laws (articles 138, 139 and 213) ensured that no news attacking
the Empire and its subjects was published, otherwise they would be indef-
initely suspended. In 1862, a *Matbuât Müdürlüğü* ("Administration of
Press Affairs") was established. One year before (1861), the first private and
independent Ottoman-Turkish newspaper *Tercüman-ı Ahval* was funded
and published by Agâh Effendi. The newspaper was also the first Ottoman
press to be suspended by the state due to a clash of ideas with *Ceride-i
Havadis* and increasing competition between the two newspapers.

The expansion of independent publications in the following decades and
criticism of the state by *Tercüman-ı Ahval* and *Tasvir-i Efkar* ("Depiction
of Ideas", the second independent Ottoman-Turkish newspaper) led to the
first press law enacted by the government in December 1864 (an adaptation of the 1852 Press Law of Louis Napoléon Bonaparte) and remaining
in place until the 1909 constitutional revolution. These punitive censorship laws aimed to control and prevent non-conformist ideas in existing
publications and their dissemination among the elite and the public. In
broader terms, the law introduced licensing for all political publications,
prohibited inappropriate remarks and controlled the content and criticism
about the sultan and state policies; punishments such as imprisonment,
monetary penalties and suspension of publication were implemented to
enforce this. The control mechanisms of the press were tightened further in
1867 with a temporary law named *Kararname-i Ali*, which allowed for the
suspension of newspapers such as *Muhbir* ("The Informer") and *Tasvir-i
Efkar* without trial for "the best interests of the state" (qtd in Baykal
23). Originally, this law was claimed to have been developed in order to
"silence the movement against Sultan Abd[u]laziz" (24). This movement
was triggered by an organisation named the Young Ottomans, an activist
group that asked for a new constitution and a parliamentary government
(which occurred in 1865 and was made illegal in 1867). *Muhbir* was
re-established in London in 1867 as the first Ottoman-Turkish newspaper
published abroad and it promoted the foundation of a parliament named
Büyük Meşveret Meclisi ("Grand Counselling Assembly") (Topuz 40–41).

During the reign of Abdulhamid II between 1876 and 1909, press censorship was more carefully carried out, along with his active involvement

in creating a body of publications that appealed to the sultan and the state (Baykal 24). This increased the number of printed materials between 1885 and 1908, with up to 70 new periodicals and newspapers, the majority of which expressed their gratitude to the sultan in their introductions ("mukaddime"). In the first Ottoman Constitution, the freedom of expression by the press was protected by Abdulhamid II with a statement as follows: "The press is free within the limits of law" (Yosmaoğlu 19). However, despite all the censorship policies in the Empire, foreign publications of the opposition press were illegally transferred from Europe into the Empire and disseminated among the public and intellectuals.[7] Regarding the problem of "smuggled publications", the government issued a decree on 17 April 1876 and ordered a "certificate of approval" as well as the examination of all foreign publications (19). Stamp taxes were also imposed on each published copy of a newspaper. Foreign publications were considered dangerous for the welfare of the state since they could generate support from the public for the constitutional movement. Therefore, just before the constitutional revolution, the period witnessed both "the Hamidian press" and "the opposition press", as well as strict censorship policies in the country (Baykal 28).

After the Law of Printing Presses of 1888, both punitive and preventive censorship practices were carried out and most publications were expected to support the state policies rather than criticising them (Yosmaoğlu 25). The proofs of all daily newspapers were first checked by the editor, and then sent to the censor's office for a double check prior to publication. The practice of book burning in the period is also disclosed in two official documents dated to 1901 and 1902, showing that a total of 29,681 printed materials were burned for being dangerous, unlicensed, or prohibited in the empire (qtd in Demirkol 190–1). In order to prevent the smuggling of newspapers into the Empire, the Ministry of Foreign Affairs

---

7 Censorship most obviously affects the domestic author but in addition may hinder the influx of foreign ideas through the censorship of foreign works and the control of translation. Censorship, therefore, not only limits what can be disseminated within a state but may also try to influence the information flow in and out of a country in order to protect both the status quo internally and the state's reputation abroad (O'Learly et. al. 18).

sent verbal notes to the embassies of relevant countries to stop the transfer from post offices by specifying the title, date and number of prohibited publications (27). The constitutional revolution in July 1908 by the Young Turks provided press freedom within the limits of law and the number of new publications and newspaper licences obtained in the period showed a dramatic increase (Baykal 26). However, this boom era was partly unsuccessful since the revolution had taken place unexpectedly and the rush was "completely unplanned, impulsive and opportunistic" (33). The press boom was mostly effective in wealthy and populous cities, such as Istanbul, Izmir, Thessaloniki, Beirut, Damascus, Aleppo and Jerusalem. The number of publications significantly decreased seven months after the reinstatement of the constitution and many of them gradually failed due to financial difficulties and competition over readership. The censorship laws of 1864 lost their validity and application after the re-declaration of the Constitution, except the ones on obtaining a publishing permit, and they were replaced in 1909 with a more independent form of press freedom that was effective until the Second World War.

5.3.1 The Servet-i Fünûn Movement and Halit Ziya

The relationship between the history of the press and the novel genre during the imperial decline discloses itself in the *Servet-i Fünûn Journal* ("The Wealth of Knowledge") as a literary movement in early modern Turkish literature. This movement marks a clear break with the traditional norms of Ottoman literature, moving towards a Westernised literature with serialised novels and short stories. The movement (also named "Edebiyat-ı Cedide") began with Tevfik Fikret's editorship of the journal on 9 February 1896 and many contributions from authors and poets, who had a significant influence on the formation and evolution of Turkish literature (Kılıç Gündoğdu 1). Among this group of men of letters were Tevfik Fikret, Cenap Şehabettin, Hüseyin Suat, Ali Ekrem, Süleyman Nazif, Faik Ali, Halit Ziya Uşaklıgil, Mehmet Rauf, Hüseyin Cahit and Ahmet Şuayb. A significant representative of the movement, Recaizâde Mahmud Ekrem taught new courses and wrote course books at Galatasaray High School and Mekteb-i Mülkiye ("School of Political Science") and guided his students to intellectual productions in *Servet-i Fünûn*. The young generation had a good command of French language and literature, and their translations from French literature into Ottoman-Turkish were published in the journal. They used ancient Persian and Arabic words corresponding to new images and words in their works, and therefore, formed a new understanding of language and art in the period. Their literary works mostly appealed to Westernised upper-class circles with their figurative and poetic language and themes. This understanding, however, gradually led to some discrepancies among the intellectuals within the movement. To illustrate, Ahmet Mithat, Hüseyin Rahmi and Ahmet Rasim supported a more simplistic language in the interest of the public, whilst accusing the others of being imitators of Western literature. The *Servet-i Fünûn* journal was censored in 1901 following the publication of an essay entitled "Literature and Law" translated from French by Hüseyin Cahit. The journal was re-issued after six months, yet very few men of letters contributed again to the journal.

Contrary to the gradual transition from romanticism to realism in line with the changing social, cultural and political conditions in Europe, such a transitional period does not exist in modern Turkish literature since Turkish intellectuals gained access to Western literary forms such as the novel genre and plays all at the same time (Kılıç Gündoğdu 3). For this reason, in Turkish novels published after the 1870s, it is possible to trace both romantic and realist influences of eighteenth- and nineteenth-century Western literature. In the period, the Turkish novel evolved in two different ways: it was either a synthesis of the Western novel and Turkish folk tales, or a complete adoption of European conventions of literary forms. Ahmet Mithat's novels belong to the first group and in his works the transmission of ideas and information to the public is prioritised, while a simplistic language is adopted for a wider readership. The second approach starts with the novels of Namık Kemal, who utilised romanticism and poetic language. This approach was followed by realist literary works in the 1880s, such as Halit Ziya Uşaklıgil's *Sefile* (1886) and *Mai ve Siyah* (1896–97), Sami Paşazâde Sezai's *Sergüzeşt* (1888), Nabizâde Nazım's *Zehra* (1896) and Recaizâde Mahmud Ekrem's *Araba Sevdası* (1898). These late-nineteenth-century novels reflect the characters' inner worlds and depict social life while refraining from explicit criticism of social and political issues due to censorship practices in the period. They also include many observations about ordinary people and their everyday lives. In a large number of the novels, Istanbul is used as the setting since it was the capital and cultural centre of the Empire. One of the most criticised aspects of these novels is their poetic and figurative language and complicated style due to the use of ancient Arabic and Persian words. Since this method resulted in some difficulties of interpretation by the reader, a number of authors edited their works and began to use a more simplified language and style after the 1920s.

Halit Ziya Uşaklıgil (1867–1945) is known as one of the leading representatives of the *Servet-i Fünûn* movement and the first upholder of the novel genre in its contemporary European form in modern Turkish literature. Halit Ziya was taught French at a school in İzmir and was interested in French literature from an early age, which had a profound influence on his novels and literary career. His first visit to Paris in 1889 increased his affection for the French culture and intellectual movements in Europe. His literary works contain elements that reveal this French influence as well. In 1884, the author and his friend Tevfik Nevzat established a journal named *Nevruz* and soon after his first novels and short stories were published in *Hizmet* and *Ahenk* (Parlatır 87–9). He joined the *Servet-i Fünûn* journal as a writer in 1896, which marks a major step in his literary career. This avant-garde journal aimed at informing the reader about social, cultural and intellectual movements in Europe. Following the publication of a few prose poems and short tales in the journal, Halit Ziya wrote his masterpiece *Mai ve Siyah* ("The Blue and the Black"), the story of a young advocate of the new literature. The novel was serialised from 1896–1897 in the journal and published in book format in 1898.

As a prolific author, Halit Ziya wrote eight novels, seventeen novellas, three plays, one memoir, two prose poems, six books of literary history and essays, along with numerous translations from French into Turkish in his lifetime. The publication order of his novels is as follows: *Sefile* (1885), *Nemide* (1887–88), *Bir Ölünün Defteri* (1890–91), *Ferdi ve Şürekâsı* (1894), *Mai ve Siyah* (1896–97), *Aşk-ı Memnu* (1900), *Kırık Hayatlar* (1901) and *Nesl-i Ahir* (1909).[8] In one of his essays on

---

8 For more information see Kerman and Huyugüzel 529.

literature, Ahmet Hamdi Tanpınar argues that the modern Turkish novel begins with Halit Ziya in a real sense (275–8). His novels and short stories represent the mature stage of the Servet-i Fünûn movement. He is described as a talented novelist who mastered characterisation and devising plots. In order to understand his position in the new literature, it is necessary to read the Turkish novels of the period in order. The abrupt transition from underdeveloped essays to his well-structured novels in the late 1880s reveals his advanced narrative style and distinctive quality in fiction. Although he focuses on the individual rather than critical social issues of the period, his literary style and form still capture his surroundings.

In his non-fictional book *Hikâye* (1891), Halit Ziya provides a brief history of fictional prose (story and novel) as an underdeveloped genre in Turkish literature and a critical assessment of low-quality translations from popular literature. The author strongly opposes the definition of story or novel as simply a description of events and he focuses on its more complicated nature and structure. He argues that writers can reveal all aspects of individuals, and therefore, stories and novels mirror both humanity and the human life (Tüzer 53). At the same time, he draws attention to the difference between story-writing and fairy tales, and a misunderstanding among men of letters who consider the two genres the same or equal in Ottoman literature. With a particular reference to Balzac, Flaubert, the Goncourt Brothers, Emile Zola and Alphonse Daudet, he introduces realism (naturalism) in Western literature and contributes to its adaptation into Turkish literature with his explanatory notes on its objectives and function in the novel genre. In story-writing, Halit Ziya uses a method that links causes to results in his plot and enriches his narrative with his psychological analyses. For romanticism, he uses examples from authors such as Victor Hugo, Alexandre Dumas, George Sand and Feuillet. Whilst realists analyse causes in detail and present them objectively in order to reach a result, romantics fictionalise the plot or causes according to a preconceived result. To sum up, Halit Ziya suggests that an unwanted result is preferable to an unreal dream and he supports realism over romanticism in his search for the truth (54). The psychological depth of his fictional works is disclosed in his analysis of personal conflicts in individuals' worlds in novels such as *Mai ve Siyah*.

6. Literary Analysis of Late-Nineteenth Century Novels

6.1 *Mai ve Siyah* by Halit Ziya Uşaklıgil

Mai ve Siyah (1896–97) is a canonical novel that draws upon the transformation of art and literature, and the press and publication culture in the Ottoman Empire during the last decades of the nineteenth century.[9] Ahmet Cemil, the protagonist in the novel, is a young middle-class intellectual with aspirations and ideals, and a spokesman for the Servet-i Fünûn movement in modern Turkish literature. After his father's death, Ahmet Cemil assumes responsibility for looking after his family and faces both financial difficulties and heavy working conditions. He works as a writer at the *Mir'at-ı Şuun* newspaper, as well as working as a freelance translator and private tutor. Due to his busy schedule and long working hours, he hardly has time to pursue his dream of writing poems in a new poetic language. Ahmet Cemil's relations with other writers and his dialogues with his best friend, Hüseyin Nazmi, disclose his views on the modernisation of the Turkish language and literature. The young poet translates popular and cheap novels and stories from French into Ottoman-Turkish and in this way provides a critique of popular culture that devalues art and literature. After he completes his new poems and reads them to a small group of artists and critics, their disguised disapproval or dislike of his new style draws attention to the reception of new literary approaches in the period. Ahmet Cemil's experiences in the printing house further highlight issues such as press censorship and the problematic conditions of the publishing houses in İstanbul. Literary and press censorship, the

---

9 The novel was originally written in Ottoman-Turkish and published as a book in Arabic letters in 1898 by Âlem Publishing House. In 1938, the author revised the novel by using the Latin alphabet and simplifying the language by substituting Arabic and Persion words with Turkish words. In this study, a contemporary Turkish edition of the novel (based on the 1938 edition) published in 2016 by Can Publishing has been used. All translations from the original Turkish into English (*Mai ve Siyah* and *Kırk Yıl*) are my own.

economic and aesthetic concerns of the artist, and the commodification of art and literature are clearly articulated in the novel through symbolism and a realistic representation of relations in the press and literary circles.

Symbolism plays a significant role in the transmission of individual ideas and emotions in the novel. First, the title *Mai ve Siyah* ("The Blue and the Black") is based on a symbolic use of colours, which bears some resemblance to *Le Rouge et le Noir* (1830; "The Red and the Black") by Stendhal, a French novelist whose works of fiction mark the transition from romanticism to realism in French literature. In his autobiography *Kırk Yıl* (2017; "Fourty Years"), Halit Ziya confirms his earlier knowledge of Stendhal and his novels, along with other French writers such as Goncourt, Zola and Daudet (139). He was also influenced by the French symbolist literary movement developing in the 1880s and he creatively used it in his fiction. Diverting from the romantic tradition of entitling his novel with the name of his protagonist, Stendhal used the juxtaposition of the two colours to represent the French military and the clergy (the Catholic Church). The novel is about Julien Sorel, a young and ambitious man who uses seduction as a means of achieving success, oscillating between choosing a career in the army and joining the clergy, and thereby facing only two choices: wearing the red or the black. Dissimilarly, in *Mai ve Siyah*, the colours blue and black represent the rise and fall of a young man and his dreams and disappointments. In terms of their plot and characterisation, the two novels display fundamental differences. Even though Julien and Ahmet Cemil are both young men, they have distinctive dreams and ideals about life. The colours red and black carry political and religious implications in Stendhal's work, whereas blue and black represent human feelings and nature in Halit Ziya's novel.

The novel begins on a blue night and ends on a black night, which endows it with symbolic value. Frequently defined as a novel of disappointment in literary scholarship, *Mai ve Siyah* portrays Ahmet Cemil's dreams and disappointments as the main conflict and essence of his new poetry (Huyugüzel 63). The colour blue symbolises dreams, whilst the colour black represents reality. Throughout the narrative dreams clash with reality and in the end reality triumphs. This ending also reflects the author's realism in fiction, as he notes in *Hikâye* (2018) that the ugliest reality is preferable to the fanciest dream. The author does not just use colour as a symbol but also draws on nature, linking colours to the day and night, the sky, the sea and the earth. The 22-year-old protagonist is introduced on a blue night – with a blue sky over the black sea. The stars in the blue sky represent his many hopes and dreams that allow for the possibility of them coming true. One of his greatest desires is to get his poems published and become a well-known and respected literary man. His second dream is to marry Lamia, the sister of his close friend, Hüseyin Nazmi. He longs to own a publishing house to provide financial comfort for himself and Lamia. However, throughout the course of the narrative he gradually loses hope and none of his dreams come true. At the end of the novel, the blue night is replaced with a black night without stars, symbolising his ultimate failure (Uşaklıgil, *Mai ve Siyah* 313–4). He imagines the blue and the black night together and mourns the time and life spent between those two nights. The novel ends with the darkness falling over the black sea, only the red light of a ship shining in the night.

Halit Ziya uses figurative language and a lyrical style in the novel. This narrative style partly originates from the hero-poet character and it reflects his emotions (Kaplan 437–58). There is also an intimate link between characters and place, or the physical environment in his works (Huyugüzel 79). The author uses his descriptions of places as a means of characterisation, a technique frequently used in the Western novel. Instead of focusing on the plot, the flow of events, or use of dialogue, he emphasises the delicate and fragile relations among people and the influence of spatial relations and environmental conditions on individuals. In this sense, using lyrical language helps to convey understanding and to reflect these critical relations from the point of view of a sensitive and intellectual character. This style allows the novelist to provide a detailed portrayal of places and characters' psychology. His knowledge of painting and music help him to add a dynamism to his descriptive language and his narrative style is far from being monotonous as he often uses unconventional phrases and expressions in his writing. *Mai ve Siyah* reflects characteristics of nineteenth-century European novels for the following reasons: "the analysis of emotional conditions with all their subtleties, depictions of decorations, objects and nature through the eyes of the artist, use of an artistic and figurative language, and a strong literary technique" (qtd in Huyugüzel 82).

The novel opens on the night they are celebrating the tenth anniversary of the *Mir'at-ı Şuun* newspaper, prepared by seven young men of letters in İstanbul. This chapter not only introduces Ahmet Cemil and his dreams but also informs the reader on the transformation of the press, literature and the publishing world. The intellectuals around the dinner table share distinctive perspectives on art and literature, yet they are also part of the press and literary culture during the reign of Abdulhamid II. The conflicts between Ahmet Cemil and Raci – a literary critic interested in traditional poetry – in particular, disclose the widening gap between old and new poetry (and language) in the period. Ahmet Cemil is described as a well-educated intellectual who is familiar with Ottoman and Western literature and believes in the possibility and necessity of progress and transformation in poetry. He openly criticises the 400-year-long use of a complicated style in poetry and emphasises the significance of preserving essence and simplicity in language. Defending symbolism and rhythm, he aims to remove redundant Arabic and Persian words from Turkish poems to achieve a clear language that reflects the state of the human mind and emotions. In this respect, he is a radical and modernist poet. Language for Ahmet Cemil is like a human being: it carries almost all the qualities of a living being, and therefore, it should be examined and treated carefully. The new language in poetry should be able to express human feelings and thoughts (Kaplan 383). His emphasis on the significance of language, aesthetics and style in literature reflects the concerns of the Servet-i Fünûn movement as well. In this sense, the novel is very useful for understanding the reasons behind the modernisation of Turkish poetry.

In the novel, Raci is presented as the antithesis to Ahmet Cemil; Raci is a writer and critic who strongly defends traditional forms of poetry. The theme and plot of the novel are partly established on the conflict between those educated at traditional local schools and modern schools in the period (qtd in Gökşen 230). The disagreements between the *Servet-i Fünûn* writers and Muallim Nâcî – an old-school defender of literature – and his supporters, the latter's attacks, ridicule and criticism of the new literary movement and its members, paved the way for the production of *Mai ve Siyah*, a novel of its time and generation. For this reason, the young poet character is challenged by a counter-character (Raci) who obstructs his path to becoming a respected and well-known poet. The antagonism between the traditional and innovative poetry is portrayed through the two characters, and the narrator explicitly favours the latter. Raci is described as opposing everything new regardless of its quality. He tries to find others' faults and ridicules them harshly in his essays. He is disliked by his colleagues in the press and holds a particular grudge against Ahmet Cemil for having opposing literary values.

The *Mir'at-ı Şuun* newspaper represents an ordinary newspaper and printing house in late-nineteenth century İstanbul. It is located on Babıâli Street, a street well-known for its bookstores and publishing houses in the period. Elaborate depictions of Babıâli Street in the novel reflect its major position in the press, publishing and literary culture in the capital. It is described as a street occupied by bookstores, library frequenters and printing houses, that is, a place for the movement of art and ideas (Uşaklıgil, *Mai ve Siyah* 36). Bookstores had started to emerge in the street towards the end of the eighteenth century (İşli, "Bab-ı Âli'de Yayınevleri"). Arakel Tozluyan Effendi (an Armenian publisher) is known for establishing possibly the first bookstore in the Babıâli (No: 46) in 1876. He also published essential works by Ottoman literary writers such as Ahmet Rasim and Halit Ziya. In the following decades, the significance and number of these bookstores gradually increased, turning the street into the most important centre of the Ottoman-Turkish press. From 1900, the press and printing culture was even more established. Ali İhsan Tokgöz's (the owner of the *Servet-i Fünûn* journal) purchase of Âlem printing house and the establishment of two libraries (Şems and İkbal) were two significant developments in the period ("Basın Dünyasının Hafızası: Babıâli"). In the street, even coffee shops and barber shops were intertwined with literature and politics. For instance, İttihatçılar (Unionists) used to meet in a barbershop in Sirkeci where some government policies were criticised in whispers. People at the famous Meserret Kıraathanesi (a coffee house) exchanged the smuggled Young Turk publications and talked about politics. The street was a living intellectual space engaged in politics, literature, press and the publishing world.

In *Kırk Yıl* (2017), Halit Ziya writes about his first visit to Babıâli Street and his sense of disappointment at finding that the place fell short of his expectations:[10]

Asıl inkisar-ı hayal edebiyat ve matbuat âleminde oldu. Babıâli Caddesi'ni ben nasıl farz ederdim, orasını ne muhteşem kütüphanelerle, ne muazzam matbaalarla süslemiştim. Hayalimde burası sonu gelmeyen bir galeyan içince alay alay şairleri, edipleri, muharrirleri çalkalayan bir mahşer idi [...] orada bir işkembecinin yahut bir kasabın yanında üç beş perişan kitapçının pısırık, zamanlarını nasıl geçireceklerinde mütehayyir, yolunu şaşırmış gençler, yahut hayattan sırtlarına temiz bir elbise verecek kadar nasip alamayarak nihayet bir Ermeni tâbiin matbaa provalarını tashih etmekle akşamın rakısını temine çalışan ihtiyarlar gördüm. Cadde baştan başa Karabet ve Kaspar'larla, Aleksan'larla, sonra hepsinden daha mühim, köşede Arakel'le dolu idi. Bunlar da kitap, gazete, matbaa hayatına ırklarına ait çalışkanlık, beceriklilik kabiliyetlerini getirmemiş olsalardı acaba ne olacaktı? Onların gayret ve faaliyetlerinden doğmuş bir hareket vardı ki ne kadar küçük, ne kadar zayıf olsa bile yine bir şeydi. (148–9)[11]

In this passage, the author acknowledges the significance and role of Armenian bookstores and printing houses in the formation of a literary and publishing centre in the metropolis. Halit Ziya characterises this as a suffocating place with an overwhelming atmosphere, in which one finds relief when he or she leaves the street. After his visit to *Tercüman-ı Hakikat*, a newspaper led by Ahmet Mithat Effendi between 1878 and 1908, and witnessing the production of *gazelles* ("odes") by Muallim Naci,

---

10   The exact date for this visit is not known but it is inferred from the information given in the book that it took place between 1883–1885 (Uçman 149).

11   "The real disappointment was in the realm of literature and printing. How had I dreamed of Babıâli Street, decorating it with brilliant libraries and enormous printing houses. In my imagination, this place was full of poets, actors and writers... There were a few ravaged bookshops next to a small restaurant or a butcher, some shy and idle young men who did not know how to pass time, and a number of old poor men, rectifying the printing rehearsals of the Armenians in order to supply the *raki* of the evening. The street was full of Karabet and Kaspars, Aleksanns and, more importantly, Arakel in the corner. What would have happened if they had not brought their natural hard work and resourcefulness to books, newspapers and printing life? There was a movement that was born out of their efforts and activities, no matter how small and how weak it was once again."

his disappointment about the literary and publishing world multiplies. The first impression and disappointment of the writer are essentially connected with his hopeful anticipation about the street as a luxurious and developed place, similar to those pictured in French pamphlets. His familiarity with the French publishing and literary world leads to high expectations of Babıâli Street.

The disappointment of Halit Ziya in Babıâli Street and the press and the publishing world is reflected in Ahmet Cemil's experiences at *Mir'at-ı Şuun* in the novel. The newspaper comprises an editor-in-chief (Ali Şekib, a man who knows a little about everything), the publisher and owner of the newspaper (Hüseyin Baha and Tevfik Effendi respectively), an administrative officer (Ahmed Şevki Effendi) and writers (Ahmet Cemil, Raci, Said, Saib and Osman Tayyar). In the period, the business of printing houses and newspapers was not stable since their employees and the quality of their work were continuously subject to censorship or enclosure. For this reason, writers in particular frequently worked for different newspapers or printing houses for short periods. The demanding working conditions at newspapers are described by Ahmet Cemil, who works the whole week and hardly has any free time. Although he is exhausted by the long working hours, he endures it since he believes that he can only achieve his dreams through hard work. To address his financial concerns, Ahmet Cemil tutors a young child in Vezneciler three nights a week. However, these private lessons, in the winter season in particular, hasten his physical decline and exhaustion. Competitiveness among the writers and their jealousy is another factor that makes the press less tolerable. After working for one year for the newspaper, Ahmet Cemil expresses his disappointment in the press as follows:

> Ah! Bu basın dünyası! Bir seneden beri o dünyanın az tecrübelerini mi görmüş, az acılıklarını mı tatmıştı! Okuldayken nasıl hayal ederdi! Bugün kim bilir ne kadar gençler vardır ki o dünyada bir zevk olduğunu düşünürler ama bir kere çirkin basın hayatına girseler...Ahmet Cemil kin ve hased dedikçe hep Raci aklına gelir. Bu adam basın dünyasında bu tür yaratıkların özel örneğidir. Tashihlere bakarken dizgi yanlışlarına dikkat edecek yerde ötekinin berikinin hatalarını bulmaya dikkat eder.[12] (Uşaklıgil, *Mai ve Siyah* 28)

---

12 "Ah! This press world! Hasn't he experienced that world for a year or tasted its slight bitterness? How had he dreamed when he was in school! Who knows

Descriptions of the printing house also reveal the working conditions, routines, and role of the senses in the experience of a place (Kılıç Gündoğdu 61–4). The repeated jolts and sounds of the letterpress blocks, the smell of ink, wet paper and tobacco, the routine for printing newspapers and journals every night in the printing house, are elaborated with lively and metaphoric language:

> Sabahları yayımlanan gazete idarehaneleri en çok sabahleyin sessizdir; gece gazete basılmış, sabahleyin şafağın ardından müvezzilere dağılmıştır; yalnız postaya verilecek olanlar kuşaklanmakta, tertiphanede mürettiplerin telaşa lüzum görmiyerek kasalara dağıttıkları dökme harflerin seri darbeciklerle tekdüze ahengi işitilmektedir. Yazarlar henüz gelmemiş, tütün kokusu henüz matbaanın mürekkep ve ıslak kâğıt kokusuyla doymuş havasını doldurmamış, Ahmed Şevki Efendi henüz hücresine girip kâğıdının üstünde sürekli çıtırdayan kalemini eline almamıştır.[13] (Uşaklıgil, *Mai ve Siyah* 87–8).

In this passage, the narrator effectively draws on the senses of sight, smell and hearing to describe the printing house and the work routine. The printing machines work until morning for the publication of the morning papers and the smell of ink and wet paper is combined with that of tobacco once the writers arrive in the morning. The work schedule of the writers and press machines displays a parallelism in sustaining the continuity of the newspaper. More significantly, in another passage, a subjective view of the printing press is provided by Ahmet Cemil, who likens them to "a volcano of information", the sound of the letterpress to a "melody", the engine of the printing press to "a grumbling monster", the straps of the machine to "a snake", and the newspapers to "a flock of white birds" (Uşaklıgil,

---

how many young people today think that there is a pleasure in that world but once they enter the ugly press life… Whenever Ahmet Cemil thinks of grudge and envy, Raci always comes to his mind. This man is a special example of such creatures in the press world. He tries to find errors in others instead of paying attention to typesetting errors."

13 "The printing house of the newspaper is mostly quiet in the mornings after the publication; the newspaper is printed in the night, delivered in the morning to the distributors; only those that will be transferred to the mail are banded, and the harmony of the serial bumps of the bulk letters, distributed unhurriedly by typesetters in the printing room, is heard. The writers have not arrived yet, the smell of tobacco has not yet filled the air of the printing press with the smell of ink and wet paper."

Mai ve Siyah 193). Adjectives used to describe the printing press include "oil, petrol, the smell of paper and ink" and the "foul smell of [the] nasty lamp" (248). The people working in this place are defined as "those who earn their li[ving] at the cost of their life, in this distressing war" (249). The poetic style of the narrator and the use of the senses and figurative language in the description of the printing house reveal the complex relationship between the experience of the printing houses and individuals. With further descriptions of administrators, writers, workers, printing presses and working conditions, Halit Ziya presents the reader with a realistic image of the printing houses in İstanbul.

The printing house also triggers a strong desire in the protagonist to have his own printing or publishing house. Ahmet Cemil believes in the necessity of materialistic and financial comfort in his future. Hüseyin Nazmi's library and large room, for instance, symbolise the ideal life that Ahmet Cemil longs for, with its comfortable conditions for literary production. He also wishes for prestige and respect as a successful poet. His desire for wealth, popularity and power might be described as a secondary impulse that motivates the artist in his artistic production. His primary motive is to create artistic products and establish an innovative poetic language. However, his awareness of the necessity of financial relief in achieving his goals, including his marriage with Lamia, drives him into new pursuits, such as owning a printing house. He endures hard work and even tolerates his business relations with his sister's husband, Vehbi, whom he dislikes for his opportunistic character and mistreatment of İkbal. Ahmet Cemil's position at the newspaper dramatically changes when Vehbi decides to buy it. A labour-capital relation occurs between the two: Ahmet Cemil becomes the editor-in-chief and agrees to pay for the new printing machines they purchase. Vehbi convinces him to make the payment by claiming that he could make the printing house a fortune. This condition refers to the economic value and commercialisation of art and literature in the period. Not only newspapers but also writers were tightly tied to financial conditions. Ahmet Cemil's dreams can only turn into a reality with sufficient economic power and he believes he can become a respected literary man and at the same time own a publishing house. Censorship practices, however, posed a significant threat to artistic autonomy and productions in the press and literature in the period.

The effects of institutional censorship and self-censorship on Halit Ziya's literary works date back to the production and publication of his first novellas in İzmir. The author's first novella, *Sefile*, a story of a young woman seduced and led into a difficult life, was serialised in *Hizmet* between November 1886 and July 1887; however, its publication as a complete book was prohibited after censorship by the authorities.[14] His following two works, *Bir Muhtıranın Son Yaprakları* ("Last Pages of a Memorial") and *Bir İzdivacın Tarih-i Muâşakası* ("The Love History of a Marriage") were serialised in *Hizmet* in 1887 and published in book form in 1888, after a long delay (Uçman 191). Towards the end of the series of *Bir Muhtıranın Son Yaprakları*, Uşaklıgil received a letter from Abdulhalim Memduh, who warned him against his criticism of the state: "Çıldırdın mı? … eğer intihar etmek istiyorsan beynine bir kurşun sıkmak daha kolaydır. Menfâlarda mı sürüklenmek istiyorsun? Nedir o yazdıkların? Memleketi batırmışsın, hükümeti batırmışsın, dünyayı batırmışsın…" (Uşaklıgil, *Kırk Yıl* 191).[15] Re-reading his writing, the writer realised that he had written on censored topics with a critical perspective. Luckily this had gone unnoticed and he implemented a heavy revision before its publication as a book. Soon after, the author wrote two more novellas entitled *Deli* ("The Madman"), an incomplete work serialised in *Hizmet* in 1888, and *Dayda*. Before getting any comments about the content and style of his works, he was warned by his elderly friend Şem'i Bey to alter the titles since they might be censored for the following reasons:

> 'Deli isminden ürkmüyor musun? Bunun ismi sarahaten gösteriyor ki mevzuu da cinnete dair olacak. Bir kere bu kelime Türk lehçesinden silinmiştir. Sultan Murat'ın deli diye hal'olunduğunu ve Abdülhamit'in bu kelimeden korktuğunu bilirsiniz. O halde […] İsmi değiştirmek de kafi değil. Mademki mevzu cinnettir…'
> Derhal hakkını teslim ettim.
> 'O halde', dedim, 'ötekini Dayda koruz'
> 'Dayda ne demek?'
> 'Uydurma bir isim!..'

---

14 The novel has been published as a book in 2006 by Ömer Faruk Huyugüzel.
15 "Have you gone crazy? It is easier to fire a bullet into your brain if you want to commit suicide. Do you want to be exiled? What was it you really wrote? You smashed the country, the government and the world…"

Daha ziyade sormasına meydan vermeden esasını anlattım [...]
'Bu daha fena!..' dedi; 'Abdülhamit'in mütemadiyen genç kızlar istifraş
ettiğine işaret! Sonra, onun en ziyade suikastten korktuğuna da herkes
vakıftır...' [...]
'O halde?' [d]edim
'O halde, bence bu doğrudan doğruya hem kendinizi hem refiklerinizle
beraber gazeteyi muhakkak bir tehlikeye sürüklemek demektir.'
'O halde', diye devam ettim; 'tefrika yerini bir müddet için başkalarına
terkederim.'[16]
(Uşaklıgil, *Kırk Yıl* 195–6)

In May 1876, after Sultan Abdulaziz was dethroned in a military coup,
Murad V (1840–1904) acceded to the throne, yet his mental health soon
began to decline and, after three months, Sultan Abdulhamit inherited the
throne (Uçman 195). The novel exemplifies Halit Ziya's use of self-censorship and camouflage in his fictional work during the reign of Abdulhamid
II. Influenced by strict censorship practices in the period, the author revised
his plots and contents, and avoided the use of banned words that might
refer to state affairs and politics.

In his autobiographical work *Kırk Yıl* (2017), Halit Ziya confirms this
method and provides some details about censorship practices in an ironic

---

16 "Aren't you afraid of using the title, the madman? It shows clearly that the
issue will be about insanity. First of all, this word has been deleted from the
Turkish dialect. You know that Sultan Murad was dethroned because he went
mad and that Abdulhamid is afraid of this word. In this case, changing the
name would not be enough since the subject is insanity..." [...]

I immediately thought he was right.
"So," I said, "I will name the other book Dayda".
"What does Dayda mean?"
"It is a fake name!..."
Then I explained the plot before he asked about it [...]
"This is even worse!...", he said. "It might be a suggestion that
Abdulhamid is constantly exploiting young girls! And everyone knows well
that he is most afraid of assassination" [...]
"So?", said I.
"So, I think this means dragging the newspaper with yourself and your
friends into danger."
"Then", I continued, "I will leave the space allocated to serials to the
others for a while."

style. He states that one of the obstacles journalists and authors encountered during the oppression period was the censor officials (390). Whilst books and pamphlets were rigorously examined by a variety of offices entitled *Ercümen-i Teftiş* ("Commitee of Supervision") and *Muayene* ("Examination"), daily newspapers were under the control of officers appointed for this purpose only. Afraid of being punished for any neglect of duty, they investigated every part and detail of manuscripts and marked any words that might in any way indicate criticism of the palace or the state administration. The number of works that were banned and words and expressions avoided through self-censorship reached such a high level that a new dictionary could be created from them; they reduced the active language to a less developed one. Authors and journalists were expected to know what was prohibited and what was not, and they were not allowed to write any criticism of history, politics or religion. The use of words such as "brother, star, hill, beard, and color" was ill-advised since they could refer to the sultans and the palace:

> Birader diyemezdiniz, bir taraftan Sultan Murat, diğer taraftan Reşat Efendi vardı, tepe diyemezdiniz, Yıldız Saray'ının bir tepede kâin olduğuna telmih yapmış olurdunuz; sakal, hele boya derhal padişahın boyalı sakalına ima olurdu; [...] Hatta öyleleri vardı ki, bizler, yazıcılar, acaba niçin memnudur diye uzun uzun, üç beş kişi bir araya toplanarak, uğraşır, sebebini, hikmetini araştırırdık.[17] (Uşaklıgil, *Kırk Yıl* 391)

The novelist further adds that the censorship on language was so heavy and obscure that they would sometimes gather and discuss possible reasons for the prohibition of some particular words and expressions.

With regard to literary production, the process of censorship is carefully described by Halit Ziya in sequence. Every writer/poet would first compose their article, poem or novel within the framework of predictions and/or existing knowledge of the list of words to be avoided, and then they

---

17 "You couldn't say 'brother'; there was Sultan Murad on the one hand, and Reşat Effendi on the other. You could not use the word 'hill' since you would have suggested that the Yıldız Palace was on a hill. The word 'beard', in particular, would immediately imply the sultan's dyed beard... There were even words that we, three or five writers, would gather together and discuss, trying to understand the possible reason for its prohibition."

would inspect their work and revise it with a critical perspective. Then the manuscript was sent to the proprietor or the managing director of the journal or publishing house for examination, finally to be transferred to the censor official before or after midnight. As a result of this, some authors would get their works published in other cities in order to avoid censorship of their works. As Huyugüzel notes, it is known from the biographical work of Mehmet Rauf (a contemporary and friend of Halit Ziya) that *Servet-i Fünûn* writers such as Tevfik Fikret, Cenap, Mehmet Rauf and Hüseyin Cahit had some of their essays (that might have been subject to censorship in İstanbul) published in *Mütâlaa*, a journal established in Salonica (Thessaloniki) due to its less intense political atmosphere and pressures (12).

At the time of the oppression and censorship in the Empire, the average lifespan of journals was quite short. The *Servet-i Fünûn* journal survived only a few years (presumably longer than expected due to its critical stance) and the publication of *Mai ve Siyah* was made possible by the protection provided by Veled Çelebi, a censor official with a high respect for literature and the tolerance of Hifzi (Uşaklıgil, *Kırk Yıl* 393). Without their assistance, the journal and the novel could have never been published. Halit Ziya admits that his initial plan was to write a novel that portrayed the rise and fall of a dreamer in two main parts. The first part would describe the social, economic, administrative and political condition of the country, and the second part would deal with the protagonist's quest for love and his involvement with art and literature. However, the young author soon gave up on writing the first part and focused only on the second section. This confession proves an explicit self-censorship and illustrates the effects of censorship practices on art and literary production. The plot and content of the novel was substantially altered by the writer due to censored subjects and the writer moved away from his original intention, in some ways leaving the novel permanently incomplete:

> *Mai ve Siyah*...Bunu başka türlü tasavvur ederdim. O zamanın hayatından, idaresinden, memlekette teneffüs edilen zehirle dolu havadan muzdarip, mariz bir genç, hulâsa devrin bütün hayalperest yeni nesli gibi bir bedbaht tasvir etmek isterdim ki ruhunun bütün acılarını haykırsın, coşkun bir delilikle çırpınsın ve bütün emelleri parmaklarının arasından kaçan gölgeler gibi silinip uçunca, o da gidip kendisini, ölmek için saklanan bir kuş gibi, karanlık bir köşeye atsın. Bu gençte bir aşk yıldızı, bir de sanat hülyası olacaktı [...] Bu

esasın ilk büyük kısmından tabiatıyla vazgeçilince ortada ancak sanat ve aşk hülyaları kalıyordu, onun içindir ki birçok munsif münekkitlerin dedikleri gibi Ahmet Cemil itmam edilmemiş bir müsvedde hâlinde müphemiyetle muhat kalmıştır, fakat gene o münekkitler onun etrafını teşkil eden şahısları pek zî-hayat buldular. Bu da pek tabiî idi: Ahmet Cemil'i bizarrure memleketin umumi muhitinden çıkarmaya mecburiyet hasıl olunca onu matbuat âleminin hususi ve mahdut zemininde bırakmak lazım gelmişti ve bu zemin ele alınacak, tasvir olunacak o kadar mebzul unsurlarla dolu idi ki kendiliklerinden koşuşup eseri doldurmaya müheyya idiler.[18] (Uşaklıgil, *Kırk Yıl* 415)

Whilst some critics have referred to the high value of this literary work, they have naturally drawn attention to its incompleteness since the scope of the novel was restricted to a small community and location. However, Halit Ziya's choice of setting as a printing house and newspaper in İstanbul provided an opportunity to emphasise the condition of artists and journalism in the period. This approach allowed the author to elaborate on the network of artists and journalists, and the operation of printing and publishing houses in late-nineteenth-century Istanbul. In this sense, the novel provides invaluable insight into authorship and literary production, alongside the protagonist's desire to become a respected literary man. The author replaces the first (intended) part with a detailed narrative of the condition of the press and literature in the period. Self-censorship by the author in this way contributes to its originality in portraying the young generation of intellectuals poised between the state's orders and transforming literary and publication culture.

---

18 *"Mai and Siyah...* I had imagined this book differently. Suffering from life, administration, the poisonous air filled the country of the time, I would have liked to portray a sensitive young man, like all the dreamy new generation of the era, so that he would have shouted out all the pain of his soul, fluttered with all the ambitions of his soul, and when all his wishes escaped and were wiped away from his fingers like shadows, let him go and throw himself in a dark corner, like a bird hiding to die. This young man would have had a love story and a literary ideal [...] When the first major part of this principle was naturally abandoned, there was only art and love dreams left, so as many critics stated, Ahmet Cemil remained ambiguously encircled by an incomplete manuscript, yet the people around him were described vivaciously. This was of course very natural: when it was necessary to remove Ahmet Cemil from the general conditions of the country, he had to be left in the private and limited ground of the printing world, and this ground was so full of elements that they were ready to fill in the novel by themselves."

Mehmet Kaplan suggests that in the novels of Halit Ziya, characters such as Ahmet Cemil in *Mai ve Siyah* and Adnan in *Aşk-ı Memnu* represent passive figures and intellectuals due to the oppressive atmosphere in the country during the reign of Abdulhamid II (397). However, despite the restrictions and oppression in the period, it is difficult to claim that these factors completely hindered the artist's creativity or literary production. On the contrary, they seem to play a significant role and even have a counter-effect on intellectuals and artists' demands for their own voice, triggering their artistic production in the period. Halit Ziya's continuous efforts to write for existing journals and establish new ones (*Hizmet*), and the production and publication of many major works in early modern Turkish literature, such as poems, short stories and novels, supports this opinion. Although strict censorship practices and self-censorship were observed in literary production and the publication world, intellectuals still managed to contribute to literature and art, although with some limitations.

During the imperial decline, censorship practices on the selection and publication of translations of Western literary works were also quite prevalent. Translated works were rigidly examined by the censor authorities and either major revisions were required, or they were completely rejected unless they contained no possible threats against culture, state, religion or politics. In terms of the aim of literary translation and the translation process, Halit Ziya advocated an approach that targeted preserving the essence or core and style of the source text in the translated work (*Kırk Yıl* 274–81). Taking each author's different linguistic style in original texts into consideration, he suggests that the translator should also attempt to apply distinctive translation strategies in order to distinguish the author's work from that of others. As an experimental study, Halit Ziya translated a number of short stories from a variety of French writers with distinctive styles, such as Armand Silvestre, Arsène Houssaye, Alphonse Daudet, Paul Arène and Catulle Mendès, and in his translations, he strove to preserve their original linguistic style and equivalence in the Turkish translation. When Halit Ziya received an offer from a publisher to get his translations published in a few volumes, he accepted it and his works were sent to the committee of supervision and examination for a license for publication. His translations went through strict revision by the censor committee and some were rejected. The publisher, however, assigned an employee to revise them thoroughly and later published only accepted translations of stories in a smaller volume.

In the novel, Halit Ziya emphasises the devaluation of translation through Ahmet Cemil's experience of working as a translator to earn money. Hüseyin Nazmi dreams of translating Alphonse de Lamartine's *Raphaël* (1849) and Ahmet Cemil favours Alfred de Musset's *The Confession of a Child of the Century* (1836) to translate into Turkish. However, Ahmet Cemil's first translation turns out to be a cheap multi-volume novel entitled *The Daughter of the Thief*. Although the young poet reluctantly completes the translation of the novel because of his financial concerns, the owner of the bookstore continuously delays his payment due to the need to edit and get a licence for the publication of the novel. The effects of censorship practices and problems encountered by freelance translators are revealed in this example in a clear and convincing way. Ahmet Cemil's income is quite small since the novel is serialised and the amount of payment depends on bookstore owners. He considers writing articles for journals published by bookstores and is later directed to *Mirat-ı Şuun*, where he starts working as a regular writer and translator. His disappointment with the literary world and the printing profession is later temporarily replaced with dreams of being the leading author and editor-in-chief of a newspaper, establishing a printing house and owning a small flat and a horse and cart.

Mai ve Siyah reflects the characteristics of the artist's novel – a *Künstlerroman* – in describing the tragedy of the artist.[19] In the novel,

---

19 *Künstlerroman* (the artist's novel) is usually defined as a sub-class of *Bindungsroman* (apprenticeship novel) that deals with the emotional and intellectual development of an artist- a painter, a musician, or a poet from childhood or adolescence. The term is originated in German Romanticism with Ludwig Tieck's *Franz Sternbalds Wanderungen* (1798; Franz "Sternbald's Wanderings") and some classic examples includes James Joyce's *Portrait of the Artist as a Young Man* (1916), Zola's *L'Oeuvre* (1886), and Thomas Mann's *Doctor Faustus* (1947). Whilst *Bildungsroman* often begins with the protagonist's ideals of becoming a great artist but ends up with either reaching his dreams or becoming an ordinary citizen, the *Künstlerroman* usually ends in failure of the artist in adapting to contemporary conditions and his rejection of society and commonplace life. The latter also portrays the artist's struggles in the middle or old age, or the central character is a historical figure.

Ahmet Cemil represents the idealist poet who rejects the values of bourgeois society and elevates art over life, and for this reason, the plot is mainly established based on discussions of aesthetic and economic value (Parla 41–2). For the artist who strives to bring art to the centre of his/her life, disappointment based on the capitalist modes of literary production is indispensable. For this reason, the ultimate failure of the artist at the end of his/her quest is understandable. Real art is almost always incomplete, and this incompleteness triggers dissatisfaction with artistic production by the artist (4). The artist also has to confront the demands of the bourgeois class and the conventional family as the representative of the middle class, educational and religious institutions pursuing the middle-class ideology, and conservative critics. As the poet protagonist, Ahmet Cemil experiences failure despite his talent. The novel represents the struggle of the poet within society, the difficulties he encounters in the process of artistic production, and the conflicts he experiences within himself in preserving his poet identity (Gökşen 10).

Characterisation of Ahmet Cemil as a young poet is closely associated with melancholy, creativity and romanticism. In terms of creativity in artistic production, Bateson and Martin suggest that daydreaming allows the dreamer to distance him/herself from the present and encounter new connections and ideas (145). When facing a problem, daydreaming can help the individual find a different solution through a distinctive perspective. The night Ahmet Cemil and his friends gather at the Tepebaşı Garden marks a specific moment when the protagonist dreams about the future. His creativity and dreamworld are fostered on a clear blue night with Waldteufel's waltz music in the background. Dreams and reality are indistinguishable in this intense and complicated state of mind of the mesmerised artist and this triggers creativity and inspiration (Gökşen 282–3). The blue sky evokes Ahmet Cemil's hopes, dreams and creativity, and the black night refers to his ultimate disappointment. Since creativity emerges more easily in relaxed moments, it is not surprising that Ahmet Cemil goes through this experience in Tepebaşı rather than when he is working in his office. For this reason, he forms his poetic manifesto on this night as he is inspired, concentrated and enlightened on the new form of language.

Difficulties encountered in the process of artistic creativity and production play a fundamental role in Ahmet Cemil's life. His desire to explore the perfect language in poetry and his high opinion of aesthetic language and music in artistic production make him an ambitious poet and, for this reason, he works slowly and meticulously on his poems. However, he is often dissatisfied with the result since he aims for perfect language and style in poetry. His rigorous method prolongs the production of his poems and he re-writes and revises them constantly. In the novel, after spending weeks reading, examining and thinking about poetry in Western literature, he is able to write only about 20 verses. Although he is a talented man, he wishes to be a distinguished poet opening up new avenues in poetry. He believes new thoughts require new words. Using old dictionaries as a reference, he uses ancient words with new meanings and sometimes makes up a new word to use in his poetry. His meticulous work entails editing and simplifying his first drafts of poems, and he finally fills a small notebook with his poems. He hopes that some critics and readers will be able to see the artistic value of his work.

Soon he has an opportunity to read his poems to a small group of literary men and critics, with the support of his friend Hüseyin Nazmi, who describes his poems as a new movement in poetry. Nevertheless, the small circle are not really impressed by his poems and they shrink from commenting on them. Raci's sarcastic comments on his poems in a newspaper column are entitled *A Literary Show??!!* and his ridicule of Ahmet Cemil's new approach to poetry, along with his erroneous translations of cheap novels, leads to the latter's despair in his literary ideals (Uşaklıgil, *Mai ve Siyah* 240–1). After Raci's ridicule of his poems, Ahmet Cemil loses his position as the leading author to Osman Tayyar. He quits his job at the printing house, yet soon finds out that he is legally responsible for the payment for the printing machines. This ridicule of his work was also experienced by Halit Ziya himself, who wrote prose and was harshly criticised by Muallim Naci, a well-known literary critic of the time. Halit Ziya sent a prose work entitled *Aşkımın Mezarı* ("The Grave of my Love") to *Tercüman-i Hakikat* and it was commented upon by Muallim Naci, who stated that "looking for love in a grave is like looking for life in the dead", a statement that deeply offended Halit Ziya (*Kırk Yıl* 110).

The intimate link between melancholy and creativity in artistic production has been acknowledged by a number of studies. In his book *Zibaldone* (2014; "Melancholy"), Eugine Borgna suggests that melancholy triggers and supports creativity and literary production (176). Poetry is defined as a literary genre that requires turning to the self and analysing the soul, and therefore, it has connections with melancholy. Borgna defines this as "a mood that shall never be cut off from any poetic creativity" (176). Either as a character trait or as a psychological disorder, melancholy increases concentration and frees repressed creative skills, as Serol Teber notes (qtd in Gökşen 53). With the influence of Romanticism, poet characters in Turkish novels display a tendency towards melancholy and their poetry/literary production is generally influenced by their mood and mental state. Halit Ziya had used poet characters in his earlier stories, such as *Bir Muhtıranın Son Yaprakları* and *Bir Ölünün Defteri*, before the publication of *Mai ve Siyah*. The two characters, Necip and Vecdi, display a pessimistic and melancholic state of mind that prepares Halit Ziya for his characterisation of Ahmet Cemil as the poet protagonist. The young poet Necmi experiences *mal du siècle* and longs for seclusion in nature (qtd in Gökşen 54). He feels down and often becomes bored with everything he sees around him, including the winter, spring months, the sunlight and overcast weather.

In *Mai ve Siyah*, Ahmet Cemil is described as a sensitive, fragile, proud, emotional and skilled poet character. His characterisation reflects features of the sentimental or romantic poet, who is also influenced by the period of imperial autocracy and oppression, which is implied rather than explicitly stated. However, as Halit Ziya mentions in *Kırk Yıl* (2017), his first intention and desire for his narrative was to portray a poet character who is adversely influenced by the deteriorating political and administrative state of the Empire and his ultimate disappointment in love and in his attempt to become a well-known and respected literary man (415). As an intellectual concerned about the problems and conditions of the era, Ahmed Cemil gradually becomes more melancholic and unhappy in line with his aggravated condition (Gökşen 59). That is, at the start of the novel he is described as a sentimental intellectual with ambition, yet he is later transformed into a melancholic poet. He is a middle-class poet who has aesthetic concerns related to literary production and he considers that art should be for the sake of art, rather than written for society or for social, political or ideological reasons. Due to his sentimental and sensitive character, however, he is not to be labelled as an artist indifferent to the problems of the period and the society he is living in:

Şiirle uzun süre uğraşmak onda hastalıklı bir duyarlılık yaratmıştı. Öyle bir duyarlılık ki onunla sakatlananları başkaları için anlaşılmaz, aklı başında olduklarına kesin hüküm verilemez; hareketlerinde, düşüncelerinde, duygularında bir büyüklük olduğuna kanaat edilir de doğruluğunu kabule cesaret edilemez bilmeceler haline gelir. Öyle bir duyarlılık ki bir gün hayatı bütün çirkinlikleriyle, aç kalmış ailelerden, gözsüz genç kızlardan, beynini bir kurşun parçasıyla dağıtan umutsuzlardan, avuç açan beyaz saçlı adamlardan, çocuklarını kilise kapılarına bırakan annelerden, bir şarap şişesinin yanında insanlıktan çıkmaya çalışan mutsuzlardan, bütün o çirkinliklerden oluşmuş gösterir; insana, 'Kaç! Bu hayattan kaç!' der; diğer bir gün gözlerinin önüne bütün güzelliklerini döker; bulutların arasında nazlı nazlı yüzen bir ay, türlü renklerin yangınları içinde ufuklardan çekilip giden bir güneş, etekleri denizlere dökülmüş yeşil dağlar gösterir, 'Sev! Bu tabiatı sev!' der; bir gün mutlu bir başka gün mutsuz; bu dakikada şen, biraz sonra hüzünlü yapar ya da bir anda kalbi hem sevinç hem gamla doldurur; öyle bir duyarlılık ki bir hastalığa benzer de değildir.[20] (Uşaklıgil, *Mai ve Siyah* 56–7)

As this passage suggests, the poet protagonist suffers from a fluctuating mood and melancholy, yet it is exactly this state that triggers his creativity and makes him a poet. The use of graveyards as a real and symbolic place in the novel further refers to the poet's increasing melancholy. Graveyards also play a significant role in French Romanticism, reminding the reader of death and addressing the temporality and meaninglessness of life (Gökşen 61).

The death of İkbâl, Ahmet Cemil's sister, dramatically increases his melancholy and he frequently visits her grave for solace and talks about his troubles. His sister is murdered by her husband and Ahmet Cemil is

---

20 "Ahmet Cemil's interest in poetry had created a prolonged tenderness in him; it is such a sensitivity that it is incomprehensible to people, the judgment cannot be granted; it is believed that there is a greatness in their actions, ideas, feelings but the delivery becomes an inexcusable threat; it is such a sensitivity that one day life with all its ugliness, hungry families, young girls without eyes, pessimists that shoot their brains with a bullet, white-haired men begging for money, mothers that leave their children in front of church doors, those trying to escape from humanity through the wine bottle, makes you think: 'Run away! Escape from this life!...'; another he compliments all their beauty; behind the clouds, there is still a moon, a sun pulling away from the colourful horizon, and green mountains with skirts pouring into the sea; 'Love! Love this nature!' one day happy and another day miserable…; such sensitivity is not similar to a disease."

unable to recover after all his misfortunes. Lamia's marriage is a second major factor that drags him into a deep sense of sorrow and disappointment. Due to his poverty, he feels that he cannot object to her marriage. He sees himself as a dead man living and compares his literary work to the empty and cold shirt of a dead child (Uşaklıgil, *Mai ve Siyah* 291–9). After his disappointments, he decides to clear away everything that might remind him of his dreams and burns his poems in a stove. Ahmet Cemil's melancholy reaches its peak on the day he is leaving the city and looking at the black sea; in this moment he considers committing suicide. He gives up this thought when his mother calls him from the ship. The sunset in this instance symbolises death or the highest point of melancholy. Ahmet Cemil's decision to go to Yemen, a desert place, instead of a European country, is another point to be considered. This escape from his past and his country reminds us of the end of romantic novels in which characters either die or escape their past and the place they are living. This might also be interpreted as a symbolic death for the poet (Gökşen 6).

The scholarship has discussed Ahmet Cemil as a failed poet, a skilled poet, as a passive character and an active character. This discrepancy in his characterisation originates from the flow of events and his (in)sufficient reactions and decisions in the course of his life. Zeynep Uysal, for instance, notes that Ahmet Cemil should be considered as a passive character since he is the doer of his deeds (255). His decision to leave the country after he burns all his poems is regarded as a rejection of this passivity, since it is a radical decision that will alter the course of the rest of his life (Gökşen 62). He attempts to put an end to his romantic poet identity and his dreams by burning his poetry book. Burning the last page of the book, which houses Lamia's note, also marks an end to his dreams of love and marriage. Jale Parla and Robert Finn have suggested that the flow of the events characterises Ahmet Cemil as a failed poet. Parla notes that his wilful isolation from the life and writing of poems locates him in the category of the incomplete artist (64). Parla suggests that Ahmet Cemil fails because as an artist he betrays poetry and when he needs money, he takes the easy way out, making translations from popular cheap novels and venturing into attempts at entrepreneurship. Robert Finn emphasises the lack of response from the audience on the night Ahmet Cemil reads his poems to a group of intellectuals (166).

However, Ahmet Ö. Evin interprets Ahmet Cemil as a successful and talented poet whose artistic identity fails in the face of the commercialisation of literature in a capitalist world (272). His financial troubles and responsibility to look after his family after his father's death trigger and aggravate his condition as an artist longing for a higher state in society and in art. Even if he had become a successful artist, he would have failed in conforming to the dynamics of the competitive world as a professional. In this sense, *Mai ve Siyah* as a realist novel presents the inability of the romantic poet to conform to the social and economic conditions of the time. As Zeynep Uysal also notes, it is Ahmet Cemil's life that fails, not his poetry (218). He is talented enough to compose new poetry, yet his experiences in his work and family life increase his melancholy and disappointments to such a degree that he decides to give up on artistic production. Although everyone, except Râci, seems to appreciate his poetry on the reading night, he loses his enthusiasm for poetry following his consecutive disappointments.

With his disappointments, Ahmet Cemil's physical degradation is hastened in the years after his father's death, as elaborated by the narrator as follows: "Beş sene evvel hayata uzun kumral saçlarıyla, umutla ışıldayan gözleriyle giren Ahmet Cemil'in yerinde şimdi yanakları çökmüş, dudakları hayatının matem acısıyla kasılmış harap bir vücut... Bu vücudu ne yapacak?" (Uşaklıgil, *Mai ve Siyah* 302).[21] The novel covers a three-year period in terms of the flow of the main events and it displays these changes in logical order through cause and effect relations. Assuming responsibility for looking after his family and his deteriorating working conditions aggravate not only his state of mind but also his physical appearance and health. Seasons are used as a narrative technique that reflect his gradual degradation and growing disappointments. The dreams and optimism of a summer night at the start of the novel turn into disappointment and failure in the pessimistic atmosphere of winter. Seasons mirror the poet's dreams and reality in a dramatic way and the novel ends with his decision to leave İstanbul for a new position in Yemen.

---

21   "Ahmet Cemil, who entered life five years ago with his long auburn hair, hope, and enlightened eyes, is now a dilapidated body whose cheeks have collapsed and whose lips are tacked with the pain of his life [...] What will he do with this body?"

6.2 *New Grub Street* by George Gissing

New Grub Street is one of the most well-known novels of George Gissing, published in England in 1891. The plot is set amidst a network of late-Victorian writers, critics, editors and publishers. It places clear emphasis on the perspectives and experiences of two writers in particular, Reardon and Jasper, which discloses a clear antagonism between the old and new modes of literary production in the publishing world. At the start of the novel Jasper is introduced as a modern young man motivated by money and he believes in the necessity of conforming to the capitalist mode of literary production. His friend Reardon is described as a reserved, talented and romantic writer who writes mainly for the sake of self-expression and he is unable to compromise to the demands of the publishers. Reardon's relationship with his wife, Amy, is gradually aggravated by their increasing financial difficulties and they eventually separate. Harold Biffen is an eccentric and poor writer, who idealises writing a realist novel on everyday life. In the novel, Alfred Yule (Amy's uncle) is a critic working with his daughter, Marian, a hardworking woman who attracts Jasper. The Yule family and their relationships help the reader get a better understanding of the condition and problems of journals, critics, editors and publishers in the period. Although Jasper is interested in Marian for her inheritance, he later changes his mind. He also improves his position in the literary world with his opportunistic and capitalist approach. When Alfred goes blind, Marian leaves the city and supports him until his death. After Reardon's death, Biffen falls in love with Amy but he cannot approach her due to his lower social status and abject poverty. His completed novel also fails, and he commits suicide on a clear day towards the end of the book. In the closing chapter of the novel, Jasper is married to Amy, a like-minded woman with a large inheritance and their happiness is described ironically as a consequence of their logical choice.

The title of *New Grub Street* refers to the old Grub Street (now Milton Street) in London, a street that symbolised hack literature, characterised as low quality and cheap literary works in the eighteenth century. The street was located in north London, somewhere near the Barbican today. It was known as a place occupied by impoverished writers, aspiring poets, low-end publishers and booksellers. It was defined in Samuel Johnson's dictionary as "originally the name of a street in Moorfields in London, much inhabited by writers of small histories, dictionaries, and temporary poems, whence any mean production is called grub street" (Johnson, "Grubstreet"). Johnson also romanticised the place, where he had himself worked, by quoting Odysseus' view of Ithaca, the lost home of the epic hero (Goode xii). However, Gissing's choice for the title of the novel indicates a major change or transformation in the literary and publishing culture in England since he suggests that Grub Street does not exist anymore: "Our Grub Street of today is quite a different place: it is supplied with telegraphic communication, it knows what literary fare is in demand in every part of the world, its inhabitants are men of business" (Gissing, *New Grub Street* 9). In this statement, Gissing not only refers to the effects of technological forms of international communication on the commercialisation of literature but also the development of professional authorship in the nineteenth century. In this respect, whilst the old Grub Street is used as a symbol of the distortion of artistic creativity and the quality of literary products, "New Grub Street" represents the detrimental impact and dominance of new forms on the capitalist mode of literary production. The existence of Grub Street as a real place in London further reveals Gissing's naturalist approach to the representation of the transforming literary and publishing world. The title, in this sense, carries symbolic value for understanding the transforming and contradictory notions of Victorian authorship, literary production and censorship in the 1880s.

    New Grub Street can be classified as a meta-fiction based on its depiction of the systematic and capitalist distortions of the literary market and publishing world and the fact that it fictionalises Gissing's life as an author and the processes of the novel's own creation ("George Gissing, 'New Grub Street', 1891"). Stephen Arata notes that the novel is "about the trials of authorship", and therefore, can be characterised an "anti-*Künstlerroman*", an artist novel in which "the conventions of the genre are systematically inverted" (11). The notion of *The Hero as Man of Letters* (1841) as Thomas Carly names it, was no longer accepted in literary circles by the end of the nineteenth century. The complex networks of the literary market and authors simultaneously determined "what forms of writing are desirable or even possible at a particular moment in history" (11). In fact, the economics of literary forms, public opinion and popular taste played a significant role in this process. For this reason, every aesthetic or artistic concern in the novel is translated into an issue of economics, and therefore, money. To illustrate, when Maud Milvain asks Jasper about the ultimate value of "artistic efforts" or "literary labors" based on "the value of it all", the latter's answer is: "Probably from ten to twelve guineas" (Gissing, *New Grub Street* 181). In the production of English novels, therefore, artistic creations were tightly linked to the financial value of publication formats and public demands.

The three-volume novel, in particular, was a format that distinguished UK fiction from that of other countries in the nineteenth century. The form carried significant importance for circulating libraries during the second half of the century and constituted a large part of their income. The price of most first editions of three-volume novels sold to these libraries was 31*s* 6*d* (£1 11*s* 6*d*), while the later cheaper single-volume editions cost about 6*s* and 3*s* 6*d* (Nesta, "The Myth of 'The Triple Headed Monster'" 47–69). Circulating libraries also favoured this format because their subscribers took up the higher subscription option (the more expensive rate) and they made profits on these subscriptions, rather than on circulation. The three-volume format and policies of circulating libraries to appeal to public taste did not encourage new fictional works and sometimes new novelists themselves had to pay for the publication of their work. The format did not create a significant profit for the publishers or the authors, especially for their first editions. With the increase in literacy and the public demand, the time between the first and subsequent cheaper editions was shortened, and the number of novels published increased to a great extent, which led to a significant decrease in circulating libraries' profits. The British public bought cheaper editions of books and the number of subscribers declined significantly toward the end of the century. Whilst the number of novels published annually was fewer than 500 in the early decades of the nineteenth century, this number had dramatically increased by the end of the century and publishing or circulating three-volume novels became more difficult. In 1884, to illustrate, 408 new books (novels, short stories and other fiction) were published, and this number had reached up to 1,040 in 1889. In 1900, 1,563 new books and 546 new editions were published. For this reason, in 1894, Mudie's library and W.H. Smith stopped purchasing three-volume novels, which resulted in the demise of the three-decker format in the UK.

Before the publication of *New Grub Street*, Gissing was the author of eight published novels and he had intentionally avoided tutoring and writing for periodicals in order to focus on writing the novel. He wrote the novel in very short time, about two months in 1890 – a pace that was close to that of Reardon, with 4,000 words a day. Gissing sent his finished manuscript to Smith, Elder in early December and a month later he was offered £150 for the copyright, which he accepted (Arata 10). This sum was the highest of his publications so far and 750 copies of the novel were published by the company in the common three-decker format. After a second print run in May, a one-volume edition was published in October. Not only the three-volume edition but also two more cheap one-volume editions (one in hardback and the other in a soft cover edition) followed; however, Gissing could not benefit from these editions since he had sold the rights to Smith, Elder. Among Gissing's novels, *Workers in the Dawn* was published in 1880 at his own expense; *The Unclassed* was sold for £30 in 1884, *Isabel Clarendon* for £15 and *Demos* for £100 in 1886; *New Grub Street*, his biggest success, was sold for £150.

In terms of literary production, the three-decker format had further resulted in "padding and repetition, the adding of subplots, artificial conclusions to each volume, sensational plot elements, and relatively empty romance and adventure plots" in literary works ("George Gissing, 'New Grub Street', 1891"). For these reasons, the French translation of *New Grub Street* was shortened by Gissing and published as a one-volume novel in 1898. The Mudie's censorship on political, sexual and religious matters and preference for happy endings and idealised protagonists in fiction also restricted and framed ideas for novel pro-duction. Gissing had tried hard to conform to the three-decker pub-lication form; however, he welcomed the one-volume format after its demise. In a letter written to his brother in 1885, Gissing admitted that the three-decker format was vanishing: "It is fine to see how the old three volume tradition is being broken through. One volume is becoming commonest of all. It is the new school" (Mattheisen et. al. 319; vol. 2). Nevertheless, the old format lingered for a few more years. *The Nether World* was published in three volumes in 1892 and Gissing added an additional chapter to *Born in Exile* for the same reason. With the intention of reprinting *Workers in the Dawn,* Gissing cut "22 pages of dialogue and 14 pages of description and omitted generalised conversation from fear of being stigmati[s]ed as a 'realist' by the critical world" (qtd in "George Gissing, 'New Grub Street', 1891").

Besides that of Mudie's and other circulating libraries, Victorian censorship figured in Gissing's literary career through major publishers and literary agents, such as Bentley, A.P. Watt, J.B. Pinker and W.M. Colles. Until 1894, Gissing's contracts were under the influence of a capitalist market with the growth of the public readership and publishers as active agents in this process. Serial publications, as well as theatrical adaptations and licencing practices made the copyright issue more valuable in the period. Therefore, the number of professional writers increased, as the memberships of "authors, editors, and journalists that grew from 3,400 in 1881 to 6,000 in 1891 and to 11,000 by 1901" also illustrates (qtd in Nesta, *The Commerce of Literature* 119–20). *The Society of Authors* also worked hard to establish a standard contract format and refused the half-profits system, although the following shift to royalty contracts marked the development of a new capitalist publishing market in the period. However, Gissing did not join this society, established by Walter Besant in 1884, until 1894 and he was displeased with the idea of educating men of letters as traders after the completion of their work: "To mingle with these folk is to be once & for ever convinced of the degradation that our time has brought upon literature. It was a dinner of tradesman, pure and simple" (Mattheisen et. al. 251–6; vol. 5). Gissing wrote 27 novels; for nine he sold the copyright and for 14 he signed a contract for an advance against royalties. Shared profits, half-profits and short-term copyright leases played a smaller role in his career. After 1892, he sold two copyrights for works written on commission. That is, in the last decades of the century, the contracts of authors changed from "a verbal agreement or informal letter, confirmed by a simple receipt, to increasingly elaborate contracts that carefully exploited or reserved rights to each party" (Nesta, *The Commerce of Literature* 120).

In a conversation between Jasper and Reardon, this format is described as a "triple-headed monster" by Jasper who believes it forces authors to write lengthy narratives based on financial necessity. However, the payment they receive for a three-volume novel is higher than that for a one- or two-volume novel, as Reardon counters:

> Milvain began to expatiate on that well-worn topic, the evils of the three-volume system. 'A triple-headed monster, sucking the blood of English novelists [...]' 'For anyone in my position,' said Reardon, 'how is it possible to abandon the three volumes? It is a question of payment. An author of moderate repute may live on a yearly three-volume novel – I mean the man who is obliged to sell his book out and out, and who gets from one to two hundred pounds for it. But he would have to produce four one-volume novels to obtain the same income; and I doubt whether he could get so many published within the twelve months.' (Gissing, *New Grub Street* 203)

Gissing's novels before the 1890s were published as either two- or three-volume novels for economic reasons and due to his desire for a reputation as an author:[22] "Tomorrow I begin my new book, which will be called 'Demos'. Alas, it must be three vols" (Mattheisen et. al. 262–3; vol. 2). In a letter to his friend Eduard Bertz in 1891 Gissing wrote that: "I do wish I could have done with 3-vol. novels, & publish henceforth in a rational way. But I fear the money-question will forbid it" (332). In *New Grub Street*, when Jasper asks Reardon why circulating libraries avoid one-volume novels, the latter states that: "Profits would be less, I suppose. People would take the minimum subscription" (Gissing 204). However, this did not mean that Gissing's novels created sufficient profit for him or his publishers, Smith, Elder (Nesta 51). The publisher lost £45 on sales of 371 copies of *The Nether World* (1889) and £16 on sales of 447 copies of *New Grub Street* (1891). Bentley's loss on the sales of *The Emancipated* (1890) was £23 on sales of 497 copies. For his three-volume novels, Gissing was paid an amount between £50 and £150, yet some of the editions of these novels were not profitable for the publisher either.

In one of his letters to his brother in 1891, Gissing elaborated on the economic aspect of his three-volume novels as follows:

> A word or two about the Smith & Elder matter. A short time ago, [Morley] Roberts & I made a calculation of the publisher's profits on a 3-vol. novel, & we were startled to find how very small they are in the case of books which have

---

22 Gissing had eleven of his novels appear in three-volume editions, including *A Life's Morning* (Smith, Elder & Co., 1888), which he wrote as two volumes but was published in three. *Isabel Clarendon* (Chapman & Hall, 1886) was written as a three-volume novel but, at the suggestion of Chapman & Hall's reader, George Meredith, it was rewritten for two-volume publication (Festa 48–9).

no great success. Now the sale of my novels is assuredly small; if the publishers gave a large sum, they would have to count for recoupment upon a steady sale for some years, which of course is a matter of much doubt. The 3 vol. novel is sold to the libraries for 15/-, & even that figure will have to be reduced, they say, owing to the competition of the swarm of new houses, which offer novels, good enough to meet the demand, for 7 & 8 shillings. S & E assure me that they have sold only 450 copies of 'Thyrza.' On the first edition of my books, I believe they make little or nothing. Remember that, if I received a royalty, 20 per cent on the sale price would be very good; & 20 per cent of 15/- is 3/-, & therefore in order that I might receive £150, no less than 1000 copies would have to be sold. (Mattheisen et. al. 158–60; vol. 4)

Although Smith, Elder lost money on the first edition of *New Grub Street* in 1891, the subsequent cheap editions of the novel in the following years provided them with about £104 a year until 1903 (Nesta 52). In the novel, Reardon believes in the benefits of the circulating libraries for novelists: "... from the commercial point of view the libraries are indispensable. Do you suppose the public would support the present number of novelists if each book had to be purchased? A sudden change to that system would throw three-fourths of the novelists out of work" (Gissing, *New Grub Street* 203). First novels of authors were also difficult to sell due to their low profit and Gissing himself paid for the publication of his first work *Workers in the Dawn*. New fiction was not encouraged much by circulating libraries and this had a detrimental influence on publishers' choices. *Mrs Grundy's Enemies* by Gissing, for instance, was rejected by Smith, Elder: "It exhibits a great deal of dramatic power and is certainly not wanting in vigour but in our judgement it is too painful to please the ordinary novel reader and treats of scenes that can never attract the subscribers to Mr. Mudie's Library" (Mattheisen et. al. 99; vol. 2). Some other publishers, such as Remington and Bentley, offered low amounts for publication, and Bentley withdrew its offer "even after extensive revision and after the first two volumes had been published" (Nesta 61). Gissing links the unnecessary parts or lengthy dialogues in his novels such as *New Grub Street* and *Born in Exile* to the three-volume format, in response to a complaint by a French critic:

Of course you are right about the superfluities to be found in both of them. The fault is partly due to their having been written when English fiction was subjected to the three volume system; but also in a measure to the haste in which all my early work was done. As the Oxford undergraduate said about his essay – I had no time to make the things shorter. However, in the case of New Grub Street, this defect is remedied in the French translation; almost a third of the novel has been cut out. If ever I get the opportunity, I shall give all my books a vigorous revision, and cut them down. (Gettmann 253)

Although Gissing's portrayal of the professional author draws substantially on his past experiences, he carefully depicts the transforming "reading patterns and publishing practices" after the 1870s (Arata 11–2). The developments in the printing culture and literary market significantly altered the economic, cultural and psychological conditions in which writers earned their living through literature. John Good notes that the "fundamental motif of the Gissing novel is the condition of being unclassed" (qtd in Arata 13). Gissing's self-alienation and unclassed position in the social order and his ideal persona were reflected in different forms in his narratives, such as "the classic scholar, the polymath man of letters, the literary gentleman" (13). What Arata refers to as Gissing's "class dislocation" is renamed "class alienation" by Frederic Jameson since "[…] intellectuals [were] perpetually suspended between two social worlds and two sets of class values and obligations" (13). Reardon's gradual degradation and continuous efforts towards artistic production as a socially unclassed man of letters in the literary circle comprise the most significant part of the novel.

Gissing notes that his novel "deals with a class of young men distinctive of our time – well educated, fairly bred but without money" (Mattheisen et. al. 296; vol. 5). As a novelist at the start of his career, Gissing aimed to reach the intellectual few rather than a wider audience since he believed his fiction would not appeal to popular taste. In a letter to his sister Margaret, he stated that "I can scarcely think that my own writing will ever be popular […] a few intelligent people will come to look out for it but the mob will go to other people who better suit their tastes" (47; vol. 3). However, Gissing was also aware of the necessity of financial security and he desired both money and status as a respectable writer. In 1887, he admitted that "I want money & all it can bring very badly […] but I want a respectable position in literature even more" (135). Yet, his experiences were more difficult than he expected. With "money anxieties, domestic turmoil and the constant pressure to produce a copy" he worked very hard and complained that he did not receive the public attention he deserved: "I exhaust myself in toil – & the public pays no heed" (67; vol. 4). Although Gissing's novels never reached a large audience and level of popularity (perhaps except for *New Grub Street* and *Private Papers of Henry Ryecroft* compared to his other novels), he was considered a respectable author.

As a response to George Moore's *A New Censorship of Literature*, Gissing claimed that Moore was "directing his indignation in the wrong quarter" since the fault was English novelists who wrote "miserable stuff" and who "fear to do their best lest they should damage their popularity, and consequently their income" (Mattheisen et. al. 276–7; vol. 2). Instead of criticising the circulating libraries and the three-volume format, Gissing claimed that "If art decay among us, we must, in an age like ours, blame the artists" and to improve the English public taste for reading he called for "artistic conscience", which he believed would solve the problem of circulating libraries as well (276–7). In fact, his novel *Mrs Grundy's Enemies* was rejected by Smith, Elder for being "too painful to please the ordinary novel reader" and containing "scenes that can never attract the subscribers to Mr Mudie's Library" (99). His extensive revisions of the manuscript for its publication by Bentley also resulted in its disappearance and the novel never reached the public (Arata 18). He was clearly influenced by the popular taste, censorship of the circulating libraries and the pressure to write three-volume novels in the period; however, he found the solution in the artists themselves, rather than other mediums in the literary market. Although he criticised the economic conditions in which authors had to produce literary works, he objected to considering literature as a trade and men of letters as tradesmen or businessmen. Gissing seems to have refrained from arguing the economic worth of literature and disliked Moore's work since he likened his reaction to a businessman's attitude. When *Literature at Nurse* was published, he described it as "vulgar beyond imagination" in a letter to his brother Algernon (Mattheisen et. al. 328; vol. 3). Seemingly, he disliked taking an active role in economic profit through publication and believed that "the pursuit of money degrades", as Adrian Poole also points out (Poole 154). He wanted to become a writer rather than a businessman who considers writing as a trade; in a letter to Thomas Hardy he stated that, "I hope to make my life & all its acquirement subservient to my ideal of artistic creation" (Mattheisen et. al. 42; vol. 3).

Gissing focused on writing novels rather than essays, reviews or short stories because he believed that his intellectual idealism could only be realised through long narratives and he consistently distanced himself from practices of commercialisation of literary property. In his early novels, despite the pressing public and publishing censorship practices of the 1880s, Gissing did not refrain from writing about the life of the poor and working classes and constructing outcast intellectual characters (such as Arthur Godwin in *Workers in the Dawn*) within the context of "class, degeneration, education, environmental and hereditary theory, marriage, money, philanthropy, philosophy, politics and women's rights" (Harrison xvi). The lack of explicit expressions of Victorian sexuality in Gissing's works is another significant aspect that addresses the influence of censorship on his literary works in the period. The love between a young man and a sex worker in *The Unclassed*, for instance, was commented upon by a critic who observed the situation as "an incident hardly within the range of probability, to say the least" (Morton, "A Review on George Gissing's Letters"). The sexual attraction between Waymark and Ida is expressed through curtailed expressions and substituted by intellectual conversations between the two. Gissing described the 1880s and 1890s as "decades of sexual anarchy, when the notions of gender that governed sexual identity and behaviour were being constantly eroded" (Showalter, "Sexual Anarchy"). In *Demos*, on the other hand, Gissing made use of an expression that Cotter Morison had applied to a social chatterer in the original manuscript as "Heaven defend me from that *cloaca maxima* of small talk!" (qtd in Pilgrim 9). In the published version of the novel by Smith, Elder, however, the term was replaced with "her" and Alfred Waltham states his wish as "Heaven defend me from *her* small talk!" (Pilgrim 10). It is not clear whether Gissing noticed this excision in the proofs, since he was in Paris in March 1886, and whether he silently accepted it for the sake of publication despite the explicit censorship on his self-expression.

The late Victorian era further witnessed the redefinition of the concepts of masculine and feminine and the emergence of terms such as "feminism", "homosexuality" and "the emancipated woman", all regarded as a threat to traditional Victorian family. In *The Victorian Frame of Mind* (1957), Walter J. Houghton notes that the Victorians' "excessive censorship [was] intended to protect and support the code of chastity, or to prevent the embarrassment of looking at what was felt to be shameful" (356). Censorship on expressions of obscenity and sexuality manifested itself on private, public and institutional levels. A number of novelists voiced objections to these constraints, such as George Moore and Thomas Hardy, who believed that the rise and development of the novel genre was jeopardised by popular means of publication, such as magazines and the circulating libraries (Menke, "The End of the Three-Volume Novel System"). In the period, one of the most notable aspects of English literature was the strong presence of women novelists, most of whom used a pseudonym. Charlotte Brönte, for instance, used the pseudonym Currer Bell and Mary Ann Evans was known as George Eliot on their works. This norm for female authorship represents the impact of the patriarchal social structure on women's artistic creativity and productivity, and the discrimination between male and female writers in the period. Furthermore, in the early modernist texts of novelists such as George Egerton (Marry Dunne, an Australian woman writer and a translator of Hamsun's *Sult*), censorship was challenged through "provocative constructions of female sexuality" and public censorship was considered as "a patriarchal culture which seeks to tame instinctual nature, and especially the wilder nature of women" (Patterson 64).[23] A fictional character in Thomas Morton's play *Speed the Plough* (1798), Mrs Grundy, had become a symbol of nineteenth century moral standards. Gissing had also entitled one of his novels *Mrs Grundy's Enemies*; however, the novel remained unpublished since it was found to be morally inappropriate by publishers.

In *New Grub Street* Jasper's understanding of the "business of literature" and that "writing is a business" is an antithesis to Reardon and Biffen's understanding of literature in terms of the autonomy of artistic outcomes and integrity. As Stephen Arata notes, "the degradation of artistic and intellectual work into a species of manufacture is a recurrent theme" in the novel (35). Jasper defines Reardon as a "conscientious" artist who is incapable of "keep[ing] up literary production as paying business",

---

23 In *Mrs Grundy's Enemies* (2015), Anthony Patterson examines censorship experiences of Emile Zola, H.G. Wells, and George Egerton on controversial issues of sexuality and the ways in which these writers confronted the prevalent social pressure and ideologies.

and therefore, bound to experience financial difficulties in his life (Gissing, *New Grub Street* 6–8). After the success of *On Neutral Ground*, Reardon receives £100 and believes in the continuance of payments; however, his subsequent failures in fiction prove the opposite and he begins to experience anxiety and depression, which deteriorates his artistic creativity and production. Jasper is the antithesis of Reardon as a traditional literary man and he is not only aware of the difference between them but he also believes in the necessity of conforming to the changing conditions of the literary market:

> He is the old type of unpractical artist; I am the literary man of 1882. He won't make concessions, or rather, he can't make them; he can't supply the market [...] I am learning my business. Literature nowadays is a trade. Putting aside men of genius, who may succeed by mere cosmic force, your successful man of letters is your skilful tradesman. He thinks first and foremost of the markets; when one kind of goods begins to go off slackly, he is ready with something new and appetising. He knows perfectly all the possible sources of income. [...] Now, look you: if I had been in Reardon's place, I'd have made four hundred at least out of "The Optimist"; I should have gone shrewdly to work with magazines and newspapers and foreign publishers, and – all sorts of people. Reardon can't do that kind of thing, he's behind his age; he sells a manuscript as if he lived in Sam Johnson's Grub Street. But our Grub Street of to-day is quite a different place: it is supplied with telegraphic communication, it knows what literary fare is in demand in every part of the world, its inhabitants are men of business, however seedy. (8–9)

This view is further enhanced and discussed in the long conversation between Marian and Jasper on the role of money and social and literary networks in literary success in the period. Although Marian agrees on the necessity of money in life, she does not believe that it should be "indispensable" for an author to have a place in social circles and to get his/her works recognised in the literary world (28–30). Conversely, Jasper describes current circumstances as an increasing need to possess enough money and improve his opportunities to hold a place in social and literary circles. He emphasises the importance of marketing and recognition in the success of published works, rather than their aesthetic and literary value. He claims that influential friends in literary circles facilitate the publication and circulation of literary works and increase their visibility in the public realm. He also notes the disadvantage of a marriage that restricts a person's social life and brings no financial relief to the author. In this sense, Jasper's views are substantially different from those of Marian, who wishes to believe in the power of authors and the recognition of quality works despite their financial concerns. In a conversation with his sister Dora, Jasper highlights the role of reviews for the success and reputation of certain books, "in the growing flood of literature [which] swamps everything but works of primary genius" (456). The survival of books in the marketplace is described as "severe as among men" since the public is offered a large number of literary works in the period. Jasper believes in the necessity of ignoring ethics to gain literary success since most works will be forgotten in a few years even if they hold a high aesthetic and literary value.

Jasper's views on art and literature are also shared by Reardon's wife, Amy, a middle-class woman who suggests that "art must be practiced as a trade" (Gissing, *New Grub Street* 51). She believes that for an artist lacking the financial conditions to enable him to live independently, non-conformist literary production will bring only misery and poverty "in the age of trade" (51). Although Reardon seems to agree with her on this issue, he is incapable of doing otherwise due to his increasing fear of poverty, which hinders his artistic imagination and productivity in a significant way. While he accepts that his works are not the products of a genius artist and he does not expect a high reputation, he still tries his best. He considers most writers' efforts to be a "conscious insincerity of workmanship" to produce average works that suit the literary market taste and find this satisfactory enough (53). Amy advises him to write short stories with sensational plots that would appeal to "vulgar readers" and to see literary production "as a matter of business", however, Reardon objects that he is incapable of finding a good plot for his novels or stories (54–5).

At the start of *New Grub Street*, the process of literary production is also outlined in detail through Reardon's daily routine for writing his novels. In the time of the three-decker novel, the author spends longer narrating the story and including many details that would otherwise not be included if he were to write a one-volume novel. Reardon cannot abandon the three-volume novel since "it is a question of payment" for him (Gissing 203). An annual income between £100 and £200 would be sufficient for him, yet he finds it quite hard to complete the necessary works all in a year. He also emphasises the role of circulating libraries as beneficial since readers would prefer not to purchase three volumes of a novel. In fact, circulating one-volume novels would be unprofitable since in that case "people would take the minimum subscription" (204). His artistic creativity and productivity are seriously hindered by a compulsory word count and the completion of the work in a limited time. His motivation is distorted by his circumstances and thereby fails to drive him in creative activity. His poverty, temperament and physical degradation are accompanied by long unproductive hours and confusion about composing a narrative:

> For two or three hours Reardon had been seated in much the same attitude. Occasionally he dipped his pen into the ink and seemed about to write: but each time the effort was abortive. At the head of the paper was inscribed 'Chapter III.,' but that was all [...] And now the sky was dusking over; darkness would soon fall.
>
> He looked something older than his years, which were two-and-thirty; on his face was the pallor of mental suffering. Often he fell into a fit of absence, and gazed at vacancy with wide, miserable eyes. Returning to consciousness, he fidgeted nervously on his chair, dipped his pen for the hundredth time, bent forward in feverish determination to work. Useless; he scarcely knew what he wished to put into words, and his brain refused to construct the simplest sentence. (46–7)

This process repeats itself at every attempt to complete a volume and his continuous efforts to fill a certain number of slips every day wearies his imagination and leads to a profound mental tiredness (120–1). The necessity to complete his narrative to a deadline further forces him to worry about alternative sources of income if he fails. The fluctuating rate for writing his novels and finding an appropriate subject for his book frequently results in hopelessness and weariness that signals an "endless circling, perpetual beginning, followed by frustration" (123). The pangs of artistic production in his circumstances push him into feelings of humiliation and desperation against the commercial demands of the literary market in the period.

The novels of Reardon are characterised as works that "dealt with no particular class of society and [...] lacked local colour" (Gissing, *New Grub Street* 49). Although they are devoid of an attractive plot and flow of events, their psychological depth, well-constructed characterisation and "intellectual fervour" could still be noticed by "a small section of refined readers" (62–3). His works, in this sense, are not popular with the reading public since they are not sensational popular novels. In a review of his novel *Margaret Home*, for instance, a critic states that "the novel contained not a single striking scene and not one living character; Reardon had expressed himself about it in almost identical terms" (206). After the rejection of his one-volume novel by Jedwood Publisher for not appealing to the reading public, Reardon confirms that "the novel was too empty to please the better kind of readers, yet not vulgar enough to please the worse" (219). His artistic productivity largely depends upon comfort and prosperity since he is described as "the kind of man who cannot struggle against adverse conditions" (62–3). For this reason, he takes long breaks between his novels, providing time for recollection and mental relief. In the intervals between his novels, Reardon sometimes writes essays for *The Wayside* and gets paid for them. The first two are accepted but the third essay is rejected. After receiving £50 for his third novel, the author gets £100 for *On Neutral Ground* and travels to the south of Europe for six months. Reardon's main interest is in history and the Greek and Latin languages; however, his circumstances lead him to become an author of novels since fiction is the most common and popular literary form in nineteenth-century England. His shift to popular fiction seems to be one of the reasons for the difficulties he experiences in pursuing literary production for a living. Earlier, Reardon writes on literary subjects such as historical figures. Asking for help from a novelist in order to get a reader's ticket for the British Museum, he is advised that such essays are too old-fashioned to be successful and contemporary essays are often written either by well-known literary critics or anonymous writers working regularly for journals and magazines. Writing fiction is preferred as a source of income in the period, and so Reardon changes focus due to his financial concerns.

Gissing's characterisations of authors and the nature of intellectuals in *New Grub Street* reveals significant aspects of artistic creation, and the motives and psychological state of the artist in this process. Gissing initially focuses on the failed artist as a "refugee from despair", noting their "self-pity" (Gissing 335). Whilst for some intellectuals the degree of self-pity might lead to "self-destruction", "imaginative rather than passionate" ones endure their fate through revolt and their "dark motive" (335). Furthermore, Gissing notes, "the intellectual man who kills himself is most often brought to that decision by conviction of his insignificance; self-pity merges in self-scorn, and the humiliated soul is intolerant of existence. He who survives under like conditions does so because misery magnifies him in his own estimate" (335). Passivity is another crucial term used in the descriptions of Reardon and Harold Biffen in the novel. Biffen confirms this condition as follows: "Because we are passive beings, and were meant to enjoy life very quietly. As we can't enjoy, we just suffer quietly, that's all" (367). Towards the end of the narrative, Gissing provides a wider perspective of these seemingly passive intellectuals and draws attention to their non-conformist attitudes in the capitalist English literary market:

> The chances are that you have neither understanding nor sympathy for men such as Edwin Reardon and Harold Biffen. They merely provoke you. They seem to you inert, flabby, weakly envious, foolishly obstinate, impiously mutinous, and many other things. You are made angrily contemptuous by their failure to get on; why don't they bestir themselves, push and bustle, welcome kicks so long as halfpence follow, make place in the world's eye – in short, take a leaf from the book of Mr Jasper Milvain?
>
> But try to imagine a personality wholly unfitted for the rough and tumble of the world's labour-market. From the familiar point of view these men were worthless; view them in possible relation to a humane order of Society, and they are admirable citizens. Nothing is easier than to condemn a type of character which is unequal to the coarse demands of life as it suits the average man. These two were richly endowed with the kindly and the imaginative virtues; if fate threw them amid incongruous circumstances, is their endowment of less value? You scorn their passivity; but it was their nature and their merit to be passive.
>
> Gifted with independent means, each of them would have taken quite a different aspect in your eyes. The sum of their faults was their inability to earn money; but, indeed, that inability does not call for unmingled disdain. (425–6)

In this respect, Gissing praises their passivity, noting their imaginative and delicate natures. He suggests that if they were given better conditions and full independence to use their literary gifts, the readers' perceptions of these authors would certainly alter. Recognising their failing to be their incapacity to see literature as a business or trade in London, Gissing suggests understanding and tolerance instead of contempt and disdain. Reardon and Biffen's passive resistance is not described as mere passivity but as an active mode of struggle by the alienated artist in the face of the commercialisation of art and literature, imposed poverty and hunger.[24] Passive resistance is presented as a naturally-adopted stance by the protagonists in order to preserve their identities and artistic integrity in the city. This is accompanied by a strong repulsion for social life and a deep sense of alienation from the public. Their isolation and gradual degradation, therefore, are both the symptoms and causes of their passive resistance in the metropolis.

Harold Biffen bears some similarities to Reardon in his inability to conform to the changing conditions of the literary market, yet he is also a hopeful man experiencing extreme poverty, isolation, and hunger. He is described as a poor slim man and "a man of cultivated mind and graceful character" (Gissing, *New Grub Street* 143). Biffen's experimental novel *Mr Bailey, Grocer* exemplifies the emergence of a new literary form aiming at "absolute realism" that includes only "honest reporting" rather than attempting to have an effect on the ordinary reader with dramatic scenes (144–6). Biffen also prefers to narrate trivial incidents that change the destiny of the ordinary man in everyday life. He describes his novel as a biographical work distinguished from that of Zola or Dickens by its use and application of realism, yet Reardon doesn't expect it to be received well by critics or the public. "The art of fiction" is a term used by Biffen, who believes in the possibility of abandoning conventional fictional forms based on stage performance. What distinguishes Biffen from Reardon is his optimistic, patient and resolute character that propels his continuing efforts:

> 'I admire your honesty, Biffen,' said Reardon, sighing. 'You will never sell work of this kind, yet you have the courage to go on with it because you believe in it.' 'I shall never,' said Biffen, 'write anything like a dramatic scene. Such things do happen in life but so very rarely that they are nothing to my purpose [...] Such conventionalism results from stage necessities. Fiction hasn't yet outgrown the influence of the stage on which it originated. Whatever a man writes FOR EFFECT is wrong and bad.' 'Only in your view. There may surely exist such a thing as the ART of fiction.' 'It is worked out. We must have a rest from it. You, now – the best things you have done are altogether in conflict with novelistic conventionalities. (146)

---

24 On passive resistance in Gissing's *New Grub Street* and Hamsun's *Sult,* see Harputlu Shah 95–120.

In terms of artistic production, Gissing refers to Biffen's adverse economic conditions and starvation that slow down the completion of his novel *Mr Bailey, Grocer*. These difficulties are not self-imposed or preferred by Biffen but it is difficult to find pupils to teach and he even pawns some of his belongings for survival. His slow writing pace is not only due to his worsening conditions but also his patient narrating of a novel as perfectly as possible. The value of the art of fiction cannot be compensated for by payments, in his view, and the only point he cares for is contributing to artistic creation. His motivation, in this regard, pushes him into the creative act of writing his novel. His meticulous and original work, however, is neither encouraged nor appreciated by his friends or the public since the completed novel is criticised as "repulsive" or "utterly uninteresting" (426).

Upon its completion, the novel is rejected by two publishers and finally accepted by a firm for £15 and half-profits, which Biffen happily agrees to. Reviews of the plot and the content mirror the difficulties with the reception of new literary movements in the literary circle of nineteenth-century England. In the reviews, literary criticism on the novel form is elaborated as follows: "a novelist's first duty is to tell a story", "a work of art must before everything else afford amusement" and it is "a pretentious book of the genre ennuyant" (Gissing, *New Grub Street* 485–6). In another journal, the novel is criticised as being one of "intolerable productions... of realism" and "never interesting, never profitable" (485–6). Biffen's attempt at narrating the everyday life of an ordinary grocer is considered insufficient to suit the public taste and lacking a dramatic story or plot, as "a slice of biography, and it was found to lack flavour" (486). Biffen's passionate attempt to write a novel of literary realism fails, yet he does not lose his natural hope for beauty in the world. However, his platonic love for Amy after Reardon's death toward the end of the narrative and his unclassed status that exacerbates his sufferings draw him into committing suicide on a clear day.

Alfred Yule and his relations in the literary circles provide a picture of the multiplication of published materials such as journals, quarterlies, monthlies and the capitalisation of literature and art in the last decades of the century. He claims that the increasing number of publications decrease the quality and value in literary production:

The evil of the time is the multiplication of ephemerides. Hence a demand for essays, descriptive articles, fragments of criticism, out of all proportion to the supply of even tolerable work. The men who have an aptitude for turning out this kind of thing in vast quantities are enlisted by every new periodical, with the result that their productions are ultimately watered down into worthlessness. (Gissing, *New Grub Street* 37)

In a paper entitled *The Study*, Alfred Yule highlights the role of editors in the success or failure of a paper and criticises it for containing two opposing reviews published in the same issue. The commercialisation of literature is also confirmed in a conversation among Alfred, Mr Quarmby and Mr Hink at the Yule house. In a discussion on published materials that represent "the best literary opinion", they confirm the difficulty of finding quality articles amid the flow of low-quality works on a variety of subjects. The issue of capital is discussed as a necessity for the continuity of publication of new literary forms such as weeklies or quarterlies. A publication that would appeal to readers who "have strong literary tastes" is also considered, whilst literary weeklies are criticised as being "too academic" and the quarterlies "too massive" (310–2). At the end of the novel, the reader is informed that Reardon dies of illness, Biffen commits suicide and Alfred Yule dies in the country after he goes blind. The literary man of the era, Jasper, is happily married to Amy and he is offered the editorship of *Current* after Fadge's failure as the editor. The closure of the novel, in this sense, indicates the survival of new capitalist writers who believe in the benefit of conforming to the rules of the capitalist mode of literary production.

Representation of the city and literary production in *New Grub Street* reveals a number of significant issues regarding nineteenth-century London. Gissing uses a naturalist method for the representation of real spatial units in London in order to present criticism of the commercialisation of literature and professional authorship in the period. The capitalist mode of literary production is also intimately linked to the middle-class or bourgeois ideology prevailing in the metropolis. One of the places frequently mentioned in the novel is the British Museum reading room, which Jasper and Marian Yule also visit. In the "Descriptive Map of London Poverty 1889" edited by Charles Booth in the period, the British Museum is located in the north-west district of the city, close to

Tottenham Court Road, Great Russel Street and New Oxford Street. These areas are characterised by Booth as inhabited by the well-to-do, as well as the middle and upper classes. The place functions as a locus for reading and research by authors, editors and other professional men of letters. It is described by Jasper as "the valley of the shadow of books", whilst for Marian Yule it resembles "a prison of lost souls" surrounded by "an invisible wall of silence" and left in complete "mental and spiritual isolation" (Gissing, *New Grub Street* 107–8). The young woman loathes the reading room because she feels "an instinctive revolt against the mechanization of intellect" (Poole 143). Marian works for years as a researcher and "ghostwriter" in the British Museum reading room for her father, Alfred Yule, who describes her compositions as "a matter of business" (Severn 157; Gissing, *New Grub Street* 80). Marian in this sense illustrates the gender inequity and male dominance of the literary market, which reflects the difficulty of the woman author achieving economic independence.

Writers such as Reardon are suspended between "labour aristocracy and the lower-middle class", yet they live in a middle-class style "within the reach of the British Museum" (Goode 112–3). The reference to living a short distance from the place also relates to Gissing's use of real places as a phase in "determining their [the characters'] status, their moral stance, how they might behave" (Dennis 5). Reardon's disappointment in moving to London to pursue literary success is elaborated in a long dialogue between him and Biffen in the novel:

> [Reardon] 'I should have lived an intelligible life, instead of only trying to live, aiming at modes of life beyond my reach. My mistake was that of numberless men nowadays. Because I was conscious of brains, I thought that the only place for me was London. It's easy enough to understand this common delusion. We form our ideas of London from old literature; we think of London as if it were still the one centre of intellectual life; we think and talk like Chatterton. But the truth is that intellectual men in our day do their best to keep away from London – when once they know the place. [...] They come here to be degraded, or to perish, when their true sphere is a life of peaceful remoteness. The type of man capable of success in London is more or less callous and cynical. If I had the training of boys, I would teach them to think of London as the last place where life can be lived worthily.'
>
> [Biffen] 'And the place where you are most likely to die in squalid wretchedness.'

'The one happy result of my experiences,' said Reardon, 'is that they have cured me of ambition. What a miserable fellow I should be if I were still possessed with the desire to make a name! I can't even recall very clearly that state of mind. My strongest desire now is for peaceful obscurity. I am tired out; I want to rest for the remainder of my life.' (Gissing, *New Grub Street* 437–8)

This passage refers to Reardon's disillusionment with London. Often regarded as an "autobiography in the guise of fiction" by literary critics, *New Grub Street* further reflects a semantic parallelism with Gissing's statements in his letters and personal diaries. Having started his literary career as an emigrant young writer trying to survive in London, just like Reardon, he represents his own plight as well the cultural and economic conditions of the period in the novel. In this sense, he was forced to write his novels not only "as a creative genius but as a tradesman striving to put a profitable product into the marketplace" (Morton, "A Review on George Gissing's Letters"). His gloomy outlook on the conditions of the publication world found a place in his letters since he was profoundly affected by it. In a letter written in 1885 he wrote to his brother that "The publishers' new lists terrify one... Such mountains of literature. Yet how little of it is of substantive value." (qtd in Morton, "A Review on George Gissing's Letters."). The loss of aesthetic and literary value obviously upsets him since he observes the dramatically changing understanding and practices in the literary market in the period. Coming from a middle-class family, as with many other English writers in the period, Gissing experienced difficulty coming to terms with a lower-class living standard and outlook despite his financial difficulties experienced working solely as an author.[25] In the novel, this is stated as "What an insane thing it is to make literature one's only means of support! [...] To make a trade of an art! I am rightly served for attempting such a brutal folly" (Gissing, *New Grub Street* 51).

---

25 A broad middle-class identity seems to have been another norm, as the paternal occupations of some major novelists suggest (Dickens, Eliot, Trollope, George Meredith, Wilkie Collins, Mary Elizabeth Bradoon, Gaskell, Austen, the Brontë sisters). Some 19th century novelist came to novel-writing by large variety of psychological and vocational paths, such as journalistic or occasional writing, or sketch-writing. University education was by no means the norm among male authors. For more information, see *The Encyclopaedia of the Novel* in the bibliography.

6.3 *Sult* by Knut Hamsun

In Knut Hamsun's *Sult*, the unnamed protagonist lives in Kristiania (Oslo) and works as a freelance writer for local newspapers. His income, however, is often too low for him to support his basic needs such as accommodation and food. When he has no money, he pawns his scarce belongings until he has nothing left. His fluctuating mood, physical degradation and daily struggles to earn a living by the pen are elaborated with a first-person narrative. At the end of the narrative, the outcast hero decides to leave Norway and gets on a ship to England. Symbolically, the title of the novel not only refers to the physiological lack of food but also to the starving artist's inability to buy it, which emphasises the link between money and hunger. The effects of impoverishment, such as being evicted from his attic room and starvation, are taken a step further by his extreme isolation, and minute descriptions of his changing psychological and physiological states and difficulties encountered in the process of artistic production under desperate circumstances. His pride, self-confidence and alienation prevent him from asking for help from others and result in extreme starvation, whilst his occasionally published articles bring only a few kroners that in fact prolong his painful existence. The influence of his financial concerns, the publishers and public's demands on his aesthetic concerns, creativity and literary production are clearly articulated in *Sult*, as the artist's novel.

The novel not only provides an individualistic modernist approach to the psychologically complex human nature, starvation and humiliation but also portrays the life of a struggling author in the process of artistic production in late-nineteenth-century Denmark and Norway. In the transforming literary world of Scandinavia in the 1870s and 1880s, the Danish critic Georg Brandes had introduced European thinkers such as Taine, Renan and John Stuart Mill in his *Main Currents in the 19th Century* published in the 1870s (Ferguson 113). Brandes' efforts also established the foundations of the "Modern Breakthrough". The growing reputation and influence of Ibsen and Bjørnson in literature and the breakthrough of Nietzsche's philosophical thinking had a major impact on the younger generations in Denmark and Norway, as well as in the rest of Europe. Brandes delivered a series of lectures on Nietzsche in Copenhagen in 1888, which signalled a transitional era for modern characters. After realism and naturalism, an interest in deterministic naturalism, in symbolism and the human psyche started to emerge (Humpál 47). In his preface to *Miss Julie* in 1888, Stringberg outlines characters that are "split and vacillating" and represents the human soul as something "patched together" (qtd in Ferguson 113). His notion of "fragmentation" underlies modernist writing with its elusive and sceptical modern individuals, as opposed to the "fixed dramatic characters" of the nineteenth century (McFarlaine 81). Breaking away from romanticism, naturalism and social utilitarianism in this period, Hamsun acknowledged the influence of Dostoevsky, Stringberg and Nietzsche in his writings and he gave lectures on writers, including Emilé Zola, despite his explicit rejection of the naturalist method of portraying characters with a dominant trait. In a letter to Georg Brandes, who described the book as "monotonous", he defended his work as follows:

> What fascinates me is the endless motion of my own mind, and I thought I had described in *Hunger* moods whose very strangeness should strike one as being precisely not monotonous... My book must not be considered as a novel. There are enough authors who write novels when they write about hunger – from Zola to Kielland. They all do it. And if it is a lack of the 'novelistic' that possibly makes my book monotonous, then that is in fact a recommendation, since I had made up my mind quite simply not to write a novel. (qtd in Ferguson 115)

Strongly influenced by Dostoevsky, Hamsun preferred to create flexible and unpredictable characters that would bewilder the reader. The novel as a literary form had secondary importance compared to his ideal of portraying the human condition using a different approach and style. His approach is conventionally identified as Neo-Romanticism, a popular movement in the 1890s that focuses on "the mysteries of the psyche and the senses, intuition, and imagination" in Norwegian literature (Humpál 47). By writing *Sult*, Hamsun played an exemplary role in encouraging and supporting a radical change in literature by calling for the artist's freedom of choice.

Interested in new psychological writing and more varied and profound forms of emotions, thoughts and feelings, Hamsun wanted to use "a strong individual voice" that reflected "the modern life of the psyche" in his new work (Kolloen 36). His primary intention was to describe "mimosas of thought – the delicate fractions of feelings" and "delicate observations of the fractional workings of the soul" (qtd in Kolloen 36). Instead of creating a different character from himself, he made use of "his own irrationality and split nature, his own strong and sudden impulses" that sometimes resulted in unwanted actions (37). The first original fragment of Hamsun's *Sult*, which partly reflects his own struggles and sufferings, was first anonymously published in the Danish review "Ny Jord" in 1888. Hamsun received a ten-krone bill for the publication of *Sult* from Edvard Brandes, the editor of the Copenhagen daily "Politiken" (Larsen 32–3). However, it was found to be "too long to be printed in two parts and too short to be serialised" in daily papers and was published as a one-volume novel by Gustav Philipsen in 1890 (Kolloen 39; Ruud 243). Hamsun received 100 kroners from his publisher as an advance before the completion of the novel. Reminded that he was expected to write for the largest readership, Hamsun objected and stated that his primary intention was not to produce art for the masses. Whilst writing the rest of the novel, Hamsun again experienced a shortage of money and contacted Johan Sørensen, a Norwegian publisher, who agreed to send him 200 kroner for his next book.

Knut Hamsun himself had undergone similar experiences to those of his outcast character.[26] Although the author does not provide any background information or even the name of his protagonist in the novel, the opening lines suggest an economically-displaced migrant, who possibly left the country for a better life and was deeply influenced by his experiences in the city: "Det var i den Tid, jeg gik omkring og sulted i Kristiania, denne forunderlige By, som ingen forlader, før han har fået Mærker af den" (Hamsun, *Sult* 1).[27] Hamsun's experiences of starvation and writing as a literary career, in particular, present significant similarities with those of his unnamed hero. Hamsun had been to America twice to seek his wealth and advance his literary career, however, he came back to Europe after

---

26 Knut Hamsun was born in Vaage (in Gudbrandsdalen) in Norway in 1860. He came from a Norwegian farmer family and spent about eighteen years there. Then he moved to a small town called Bodö in 1878, where he started to write short literary pieces and worked as a charcoal burner, a schoolteacher, and a day labourer (Ruud 243–5).

27 For translations from original Norwegian into English, I have used Sverre Lynstad's translation for its clarity. See Knut Hamsun. *Hunger*. Translated by Sverre Lyngstad. Edinburg, Canongate Books. 2011. "It was in those days when I wandered about hungry in Kristiania, that strange city which no one leaves before it has set mark upon him" (Hamsun, *Hunger* 3).

unsuccessful attempts and hard manual labour. Hamsun had tried his chance in Kristiania, Norway in the winters of 1880–81 and 1885–86 and only just escaped starvation by writing articles and sketches for journals such as *Dagbladet*. His second visit to America in 1886 also resulted in failure and as a young enthusiast and writer, he arrived in Copenhagen in July 1888 seeking acceptance into literary circles by communicating with the literary elite and getting his manuscripts published (Kolloen 34). During the first three weeks of his time in the city he had to pawn his raincoat for six kroner in order to rent a room in the district of Nørrebro. He later took his carpetbag to the pawnbroker and in the autumn of 1888, he started to write the opening lines of *Sult*.

As a journalist with high ideals in artistic production, Hamsun's hero tries to maintain a self-sufficient life with his writing and refuses help from others. He oscillates between feelings of pride and humility in his experience of poverty and starvation. The necessity of writing for the masses to satisfy financial concerns contradicts with his endeavour to preserve his artistic integrity and autonomy. This conflict is intimately related to the increase in literacy and printed materials and their dissemination in the nineteenth century, which prioritised popular novels and public demands rather than high literary styles and works. In this sense, the public, editors and publishers played the role of censor, which restricted the artist's freedom of self-expression and in some ways led to self-censorship of literary productions. Like Hamsun writing *Sult*, the artist in the novel refuses to compromise to popular culture despite being well aware of the risk, yet he will not give up on his ideals. The unnamed artist maintains a particular interest in philosophy and history, and he attempts to write a monograph to refute Kant's theory on philosophical cognition (not written), and a play set in the Middle Ages (Wood, "Addicted to Unpredictability"). In his "solitary pursuit of writing", the outcast artist perceives and describes everyday life "from a unique and disconnected stand point" since he lives in a world "indifferent to his existence" (Selwyn, "Review"). His delusions, frustration and psychological hunger only add a new dimension to his artistic perception and develop his creativity.

As the artist's novel, *Sult* provides us with a good account of the frustrating process of artistic creativity and literary production by an outcast young writer in Kristiania. In the novel, the protagonist sits in cemeteries and parks to prepare his articles on various subjects for daily newspapers. Instead of using his garret, he prefers open spaces for writing. However, he is not always allowed to use these open spaces, and in particular at night, for security reasons, he is warned by park attendants and the police to leave the place. His economic desperation is accompanied by his resolution to be successful in getting his works published despite rejections by editors:

> Hele Sommeren udover havde jeg søgt ud på Kirkegårdene eller op i Slotsparken, hvor jeg sad og forfatted Artikler for Bladene, Spalte efter Spalte om de forskelligste Ting, underlige Påfund, Luner, Indfald af min urolige Hjærne; i Fortvivlelse havde jeg ofte valgt de fjærneste Emner, som voldte mig lange Tiders Anstrængelse og aldrig blev optaget. Når et Stykke var færdigt, tog jeg fat på et nyt, og jeg blev ikke ofte nedslagen af Redaktørernes Nej; jeg sagde stadig væk til mig selv, at engang vilde det jo lykkes.[28] (Hamsun, *Sult* 7–8)

His applications for jobs end with refusals and he is unable to provide up-to-date letters of reference all summer, which aggravates his financial condition since he needs to pay his rent as well. Although this urgency forces him to work harder on articles, he is unable to concentrate and produce quality work unless a sudden inspiration helps him.

> Ganske uvilkårligt havde jeg igen fået Blyant og Papir i Hænderne, og jeg sad og skrev mekanisk Årstallet 1848 i alle Hjørner. Om nu blot en enkelt brusende Tanke vilde betage mig vældigt og lægge mig Ordene i Munden! Det havde jo hændt før, det havde virkelig hændt, at sådanne Stunder var kommet over mig, da jeg kunde skrive et langt Stykke uden Anstrængelse og få det velsignet godt til.[29] (Hamsun, *Sult* 51)

---

28 "All summer long I had haunted the cemeteries and Palace Park, where I would sit and prepare articles for the newspapers, column after column about all sort of things – strange whimsies, moods, caprices of my restless brain. In my desperation I had often chosen the most far-fetched subjects, which cost me hours and hours of effort and were never accepted. When a piece was finished I began a new one, and I wasn't very often discouraged by the editor's no; I kept telling myself that, some day, I was bound to succeed. And indeed, when I was lucky and it turned out well, I would occasionally get five croner for an afternoon's work." (Hamsun, *Hunger* 5)

29 "Quite instinctively, I had again got paper and pencil into my hands, and I sat and wrote mechanically the date 1848 in every corner of the page. If only a single scintillating thought would come, grip me utterly, and put words into my mouth! It had happened before after all, it had really happened that such

In his artistic production, the protagonist does not work in a mechanised way by working certain hours in the day in order to produce an essay; instead, he relies heavily on sudden inspiration to create his next piece of writing. He constantly assures his landlady that he will make the necessary payments when his next article is published. When he is questioned about this issue, he replies that inspiration might come at any time and when it comes, he will complete his essay in a very short time. He is not the type of writer who can work regularly every day and he always waits for "the right moment":

> 'Ja, men De får jo aldrig den Artikel færdig, jo?'
> 'Tror De det? Ånden kommer muligens over mig imorgen, eller kanske allerede inat; det er slet ikke umuligt, at den kommer over mig engang inat, og da blir min Artikel færdig på et Kvarter højst. Ser De, det er ikke således med mit Arbejde, som med andre Folks; jeg kan ikke sætte mig ned og få istand en vis Mængde om Dag, jeg må bare vente på Øjeblikket. Og der er ingen, som kan sige Dag og Time, på hvilken Ånden kommer over én; det må have sin Gang.'[30] (Hamsun, Sult 306)

The psychological effects of this situation make the process of writing articles both intolerable and indispensable for him:

> Jeg følte mig selv som et Kryb i Undergang, greben af Ødelæggelsen midt i denne dvaleefærdige Alverden. Jeg rejste mig op, besat af sære Rædsler, og tog nogle voldsomme Skridt henad Gangen. Nej! råbte jeg og knytted begge mine Hænder, dette må der blive en Ende på! Og jeg satte mig igen, tog atter Blyanten i Hånden og vilde gøre Alvor af det med en Artikel. Det kunde aldeles ikke nytte at give sig over, når man stod med en ubetalt Husleje lige for Tænderne.[31] (Hamsun, Sult 52)

---

moments came over me, so that I could write a long piece without effort and get it wonderfully right." (Hamsun, Hunger 29)

30 "'But you won't ever finish that article, will you?' 'You think so? I may feel inspired to write tomorrow, or maybe even tonight; it's not at all impossible that the inspiration will come sometime tonight, and then my article will be finished in a quarter of an hour, at the most. You see, it's not the same with my work as with other people's; I can't just sit down and get so much done every day, I have to wait for the right moment. And nobody can tell the day or the hour when the spirit will come upon him. It must take its course.'" (Hamsun, Hunger 162)

31 "I felt like I was myself a crawling insect doomed to perish, seized by destruction in the midst of a whole world ready to go to sleep. Possessed by strange terrors, I stood up and took several whopping strides down the path. 'No!'

The minute details of his artistic creation portray the fluctuating mood of the artist that forces him to write on any topic that could serve as a beginning to "almost anything, whether a travelogue or a political article, depending on what [he feels] like doing" (Hamsun, *Hunger* 29–30). When he cannot come up with an idea that he can write about, he becomes confused again and feels a mental emptiness. He tries to focus on a definite question, person or idea but fails to concentrate each time. He gradually feels confused again and a feeling of emptiness conquers his body and brain. This process is repeated many times in the novel and indicates the difficulty of undertaking artistic production in detrimental conditions. It leads to feelings of outrage, self-pity and desperation in the artist who strives to find a new way out: " 'Herre, min Gud og Fader!' råbte jeg i Smærte, og jeg gentog dette Råb mange Gange i Træk, uden at sige mer. [...] Jeg sad endnu en Stund og stirred fortabt på mine Papirer, lagde dem så sammen og stak dem langsomt i Lommen" (Hamsun, *Sult* 53–4).[32]

A scene at the editor's office and his conversation with an editor nicknamed Scissors reveal the publication process of newspapers in the city. After many fruitless efforts, the writer completes an article and visits Scissors' office, yet he counters the editor's commentary on his works as follows:

'Jeg skal læse den,' sagde han og tog den. 'Anstrængelse koster det Dem vist alt, De skriver; men De er så altfor heftig. Når De bare kunde være lidt besindigere! Der er formegen Feber. Imidlertid skal jeg læse den.' Og han vendte sig igjen ind til Bordet. Der sad jeg. Turde jeg bede om en Krone? Forklare ham, hvorfor der altid var Feber? Så vilde han ganske sikkert hjælpe mig; det var ikke første Gang.[33] (Hamsun, *Sult* 150–51)

I shouted, clenching my fists, 'this has to end!' And I sat down again, picked up my pencil once more and was ready to attack my article in earnest. It would never do to give up when the unpaid rent was staring me in the face" (Hamsun, *Hunger* 29).

32 " 'Lord, my God and Father!' I cried in agony, and I repeated this cry several times in succession without adding a word. [...] I sat a while longer, staring forlornly at my papers, then I folded them and put them slowly in my pocket" (Hamsun, *Hunger* 30).

33 "I 'will read it,' he [Scissors] said, taking it. 'Everything you write probably costs you some effort; but you are much too highly strung. If you could just be a little more level-headed! There's always too much fever. However, I'll read it.' And he returned back to his desk. There I sat. Did I dare ask him for

When one of his articles is refused by the editor, he destroys it, feeling "angry and insulted, without reading it afresh" (Hamsun, *Hunger* 109). In another instance, when he finishes writing an article with satisfaction, he takes it to the "Commander", a man whose name he has been familiar with since his youth and who has had a significant impact on him over the years. His article is returned by this man, who tells him it is not on a popular subject suited to the public tastes and he is asked whether he could write a simpler narrative that people could understand better. This reaction draws our attention to the role and influence of the public censor on both authors and literary productions in the Norwegian publishing world, as Kittang also notes:

> The innermost dream of the writer is to gain access to the Literary Establishment – to the Holy Family of Letters where the Almighty Editor [...] reigns as some sort of quasi-divine Father figure. To reach this aim the hero is willing to sacrifice his own individual talent on the altar of conformity and taste. He tries to write about the subjects and ideas that are most popular at the time, and at the Editor's request attempts to remove from his articles and sketches all the traces of fever and intensity which come from his restless imagination. Behind this ambition it is easy to find a dream of social recognition and narcissistic wish for self-realisation and integration [...] The dream of the writer is once more a mirror dream: a desire to recogni[s]e his own genius, his artistic Ego, in those signs of public recognition which arrive from The Other. Therefore, he has to conform to the images of success that Society keeps putting before him, like a mirror. (303)

Popular subjects and public taste are prioritised over the artist's original contributions to the daily papers. This causes a feeling of humiliation in the outcast narrator who is aware of his artistic creativity and talent going unnoticed by editors before even reaching the public reader. This rejection by editors and publishers, in this sense, functions as a form of implicit and prior censorship on literary productions.

Considering this issue from the artist's perspective on making a choice between "cheap happiness" and "noble suffering", the former is intimately associated with financial relief without any suffering or effort and it is accompanied by feelings of shame and self-loathing for sacrificing art to basic needs and instincts (Reed 107). In this respect, real literary success

---

a krone? Explain to him why there was always so much fever? Then he would be sure to help me; it wasn't the first time." (Hamsun, *Hunger* 88)

is a noble goal for the outcast hero who sees suffering as worthwhile. Nevertheless, the issue of money complicates the condition of the artist since he needs to sell his productions to a publisher to ensure his survival. The materialistic value of his artistic creations and his resistance to conforming to social and moral order produce a self-contradictive and ambiguous condition on the autonomy of art and the artist in the conditions of modernity. The unpredictable character and unstable mood of the narrator, on the other hand, complicate the interpretation of his main objective, whilst illustrating his passive resistance and dramatic transformation in this process. In *Enigma* (1987), Robert Ferguson calls attention to this:

> As the hero's vivid torments continue, we begin gradually to suspect something that Hamsun undoubtedly wanted us to suspect; namely that what looks at first like a dogged inability to do anything about his plight is in reality a dogged refusal to act [...] We get the curious feeling that the whole thing is willed; a life-game that the hero is playing, to see how far it can go, how far he can let it go, how low he can sink, how long suffer. (111)

Towards the end of the narrative, Hamsun's hero reaches the critical moment in which he needs to make a choice between suffering in the city or abandoning his literary ideals and choosing self-exile for the sake of his survival. The ultimate decision he makes seems to be a more pragmatic one (rather than romantic) yet it also means the artist's self-destruction since his "inner revolt" and "anarchic impulses" driven by starvation and poverty move him away from his artistic ideal and determination in Kristiania (Reed 110).

In Hamsun's novel fact and fiction are intermingled and there are some specific instances that are drawn upon in the experiences of the starving artist. In *Enigma: The Life of Knut Hamsun* (1987), Robert Ferguson notes some of these correspondences, such as the protagonist's visit to the castle and his address at Tomtegaten II, as well as his worsening economic condition that makes writing almost impossible, a condition that Hamsun outlined in his letters to Johan Sørensen (111). From these letters, it is possible to trace the author's self-portrait as the unnamed protagonist sits in a dark attic with a small window and wind blowing through the walls, trying to write in the cold, without sufficient clothing (Kolloen 41). Hamsun repeatedly draws attention to the hardships he had to withstand and the scene in the novel where the protagonist wraps a cloth round his left hand so he is not disturbed by the smell of his own breath is directly related to his own experience outlined in another letter to Sørensen. In this regard, Hamsun's success had a strong link to his use of autobiographical accounts of his life in fiction, which the reader found fascinating rather than disorienting or irritating. As Kierkegaard notes on the intellectuals, Hamsun, as a starving artist, deals with his own alienation and isolation by creating art "which deals essentially with its own creation" (360).

Hamsun's characterisation of the protagonist in *Sult* is another controversial issue among the literary scholarship. His use of the stream of consciousness technique, transforming human consciousness into a fictional character and focusing on the workings of the human mind and psyche, distinguish his work from that of his contemporaries as a revolutionary, individualistic and modernist work. The central character is introduced without any information regarding his name, past and roots. Instead, his fragmented identity, self-confusion and fluctuating mood are portrayed in all their intricacies as a representation of the condition of the modern human at the turn of the century. Hamsun maintains a blurred line between realism and surrealism, survival and death, respectability and humility in the novel and switches between past and present tense, which gives it a disorienting yet absorbing quality for the reader. With an altered perception of time, the narrator oscillates between the past and the present, as one of the effects of starvation: "og det forekom mig alle rede, at den forvirrede Sindsstemning, jeg just havde oplevet, skrev sig fra en længst svunden Tid, kanske et Aar eller to tilbage, og var saa smaat i Færd med at udviskes af min Erindring" (Hamsun, *Sult* 32).[34] His sense of place also changes at times: "lidt efter lidt fik jeg en forunderlig Fornemmelse af at være langt borte, andre Steder henne, jeg havde en halvt ubestemt Følelse af, at det ikke var mig, som gik der paa Stenfliserne og dukked mig ned" (17–8).[35] Hamsun's hero lives in a repeated cycle of writing, starvation

---

34 "It now seemed to me that the confused state of mind I had just experienced belonged to a time long past, perhaps a year or two ago, and was slowly getting erased from my memory" (Hamsun, *Hunger* 23).

35 "An odd sensation of being far away, in some other place; and vaguely feel that it isn't me who is walking there on the flagstones with bowed head" (Hamsun, *Hunger* 13).

and impoverishment, which reflects the very experience of living and the condition of the artist. In *Sult*, the protagonist leads the plot and has a memory of his past experiences in each section (Wood, "Addicted to Unpredictability"). He is different from types or characters with a dominant trait, representing public morality or other values. Hamsun explains the concept behind his narrator as follows: "This 'I' is no ordinary person, no type; he is a [...] finely tuned, strange, sensitive, impressionable nature; for that reason his almost constantly abnormal state causes him to succumb to hunger and go downhill in every way" (Hamsun, *Briefe* 87). In the novel, unity and coherence are intentionally distorted by a character whose lies, pride, confessions, humility and unpredictability mirror the unstable minds and souls of human beings.

The main traits of this solitary writer bear some significant similarities to Hamsun himself, who was regarded as a strange and unpopular man in his surroundings. Hamsun was himself obsessed with unpredictability, self-confidence and pride in his everyday life. He was also known for gambling, drinking heavily, and extravagant reactions (Wood, "Addicted to Unpredictability"). His anarchist approaches, political leanings and sympathy for Nazism only increased his isolation and outcast status in both Norway and the rest of Europe. However, in his novel, the author encourages the reader to question charity as a blast of "egotism and self-flattery" and pride as "both a choice and a compulsion" (ibid). When he offers money to a tramp and is declined, he becomes very angry despite his own need and starvation. Some of his reactions to suffering, committing sin, starvation, pride and humility have also been considered as a criticism of Christian values. His frequent reference to God in moments of extreme starvation and suffering, in particular, relates to his battle with religious faith in existence, martyrdom and the punishment of human beings on Earth. In one instance he states that "And God sat up in his heaven keeping a watchful eye on me, making sure that my destruction took place according to all the rules of the game, slowly and steadily, with no letup" (Hamsun, *Hunger* 45). At another moment on a successful day, he exclaims that:

Denne strålende Følelse af at være kommet ovenpå henrykte mig og gjorde mig taknemlig mod Gud og Alverden, og jeg knæled ned ved Sengen og takked Gud med høj Røst for hans store Godhed mod mig denne Morgen. Jeg vidste

det, å, jeg vidste det, at den Raptus af Inspiration, jeg just havde gennemlevet
og skrevet ned, var en vidunderlig Himlens Gærning i min Ånd, et Svar på
mit Nødråb igår. Det er Gud! det er Gud! råbte jeg til mig selv, og jeg græd af
Begejstring over mine egne Ord [...]³⁶ (Hamsun, *Sult* 61-2)

Regarding authorship, the issues of anonymity and the preoccupation with
making a name also played a significant role in Hamsun's life (Ferguson
99). The author initially changed his name from Knud Pedersen to Knut
Peterson, then to Knut Pederson Hamsund, Knut Hamsund and finally to
Knut Hamsun. In *Sult*, the name of Hamsun's outcast protagonist is not
stated; the first part of the novel was published in *Ny Jord* anonymously
and it remained unknown until Hamsun's authorship was referred to in
the literary circles of Copenhagen and Norway. Nevertheless, the idea of
becoming a famous and respected author had always been a passion of his.
The reason for his anonymity in the publication of *Sult* was in fact to create
more excitement and surprise when his name became public knowledge.
In a letter to his friend Frydenlund, Hamsun writes that:

> The piece that was in *Ny Jord* is actually just a part of a whole. I had to publish
> it early for the sake of the money. The whole ... will be published anonymously.
> So you must not mention it to anyone ... But I will never admit publicly that it
> was I who wrote it ... But I permit myself to think it will cause a nice little stir
> when it comes. (qtd in Ferguson 100-1)

After this success, he was swiftly introduced into the literary circles of the
Danish and Norwegian writers, editors and publishers. The novel brought
the fame he longed for, yet he was still possessed with a strong desire to
pursue the psychological novel form and he disregarded the interest and
support of the public for his survival as an author. Hamsun was aware of
the significance of *Sult* in his literary career and pleased with his reception
in the literary world, however, he wished only for "the deserved fame, the
warranted respect", rather than the delusion of local fame (107).

---

36 "This glorious feeling of having come out on top enchanted me, making me
grateful to God and everyone, and I kneeled down by the bed and thanked God
in a loud voice for his great goodness toward me this morning. I knew – oh
yes, I knew that the exalted moment and the inspiration I had just experienced
and written down was a wonderful work of heaven in my soul, an answer to
my cry of distress yesterday. 'It's God! It's God!' I cried to myself, and I wept
from enthusiasm over my own words..." (Hamsun, *Hunger* 32)

After its quick recognition as a literary masterpiece among the Danish and Norwegian literary circles, *Sult* was first translated into English (as "Hunger") by George Egerton (also known as Mary Dunne) in 1899, by Robert Bly in 1967, and lastly by Sverre Lynstad in 1996. The first English enthusiast to translate the novel into English is known to be Egerton and Hamsun was initially pleased to accept her offer (Ferguson 117). However, since she could not find a publisher for her translation, the project was suspended for a time. The novel was also well-received in Germany and it was translated into German soon after, which increased Hamsun's reputation in the country. In "Translator's Trap", Sverre Lyngstad draws attention to the issue of mistranslations and implicit censors through textual cuts in the published version of Egerton's translation in America in 1920 as follows:

> If the narrator of Knut Hamsun's *Hunger* could have foreseen the abuse his story would suffer at the hands of translator and/or publishers, his demonic rebellion would surely have been considerably heightened. Curiously, the 1899 rendering by George Egerton [...] is, in terms of its general correctness, superior to Robert Bly's version of 1967 [...] However, when Egerton's translation was published in America in 1920, her text had been expurgated of all explicitly sexual content. Consequently, segments of Part Three and Four, specifically those presenting the story of the narrator's abortive rendezvous with Ylagali [Part Three] and his voyeuristic description of the sexual encounter between his landlady and the young lodger [Part Four] were eliminated.[37] (219)

This passage is significant for a number of reasons. The intervention of translators and publishers in the target text might distort the aims and essence of the source text. *Sult* is a difficult text to translate due to its extensive vocabulary, variety of idioms and expressions, stylistic difficulties and psychological depth. Achieving a linguistic and semantic equivalency in the target language and facilitating its readability poses a significant challenge to the translators. A creative misreading of the source text or an inadequate command of the source language might also have resulted in crucial differences among the translations of Egerton, Bly and Lyngstad. The translation of Lyngstad is currently regarded as the best contemporary

---

37 See Knut Hamsun. *Hunger*. Translated by George Egerton. London, Leonard Smithers, 1899; Knut Hamsun. *Hunger*. Translated by Robert Bly. New York, Farrar, Straus and Giroux, 1967; Knut Hamsun. *Hunger*. Translated by George Egerton. New York, Alfred A. Knopf, 1920.

interpretation of the text. Not only the choices made by the translators in the translation process but also revisions made by editors and publishers suggest a form of implicit/prior censorship in the literary and publishing world. In this context, the omission of sexual contents from Egerton's version of 1920 is possibly a result of a social censor, since obscenity had been a censored subject in literary works for many centuries. Lyngstad, in this sense, gives numerous detailed examples of how the original text has been distorted through misrepresentations of places, textual additions and cuts, and semantic shifts in the target text. These interventions are part of an intentional or involuntary censor practiced upon Hamsun's masterpiece and they devalue his artistic creation without his consent.

Regarding the issue of censorship and Knut Hamsun, this study considers it necessary to briefly mention his experiences in the twentieth century as an established modernist writer in Norway and Europe. In 1921, Hamsun won a Nobel Prize for his novel *The Growth of the Soil* (1917), which confirmed his place as one of the greatest representatives of modern Norwegian literature. He was praised by Thomas Mann and recommended by Ernest Hemingway, Herman Hesse and André Gide. In 1902, the union of Norway and Sweden had ended and the country had taken full control for the first time after six centuries (Petersen 1739). In the independent Norway, institutional censorship did not play a major role, whereas some implicit forms were still practiced in relation to political, religious and moral issues. Arnulf Øverland's *Kristendommen: den tiende landeplage* (1933; "Christianity: The Tenth Plague") was accused in court of blasphemy and the publication of Didrik Brochmann's *Med norsk skib i verdenskrigen* (1928; "On a Norwegian Ship in the World War") was prohibited until 1960. After the German invasion of Norway in the Second World War (on 9 April 1940), the Nazis took control of the country and implemented strict censorship practices until the surrender of Germany on 7 May 1945 (Chapman 1740).

In the post-war era, Hamsun was criticised for his sympathy for Nazism and anti-Semitism in Norway and European countries. His explicit support and collaboration with the Nazis from the 1930s onwards was based on his hope of the elimination of communism and his anti-Semitic ideologies (Petersen 1741). Due to his political stance and sympathies, his books were widely censored or burnt in the post-war period. In 1946, the 86-year old

Hamsun was on trial for treason and he was sentenced to pay the sum of 325,000 crowns in 1948 (Larsen 1942–4). The reception of his authorship and literary works was profoundly influenced by the Norwegians' strong opposition and reactions to his political identity. Censorship applied to his books reflects the public's inability to distinguish his literary genius from his political ideologies during and after the Second World War. The ambivalent effects of Hamsun's tendency to sympathise with the Nazis was observed in some European countries as well. In Germany, he was very well received when he visited the country in January 1931 with his wife and son (Boyd, "Literary Fascists of the 1930s, Great and Small"). However, a study on the reception of Knut Hamsun's works in the Romanian printed press between 1902 and 1989 reveals that the interest in Hamsun had considerably diminished during the post-war period in communist Romania, unlike the most prolific period for his publications from 1921–1938 (Lâtug 53). Hamsun's experiences and the censorship of his works show that reactions to an author based on his personality traits, religion, moral values or political stance might result in judgement of his authorship and intervention with his artistic independence and literary production, impacting the publication and dissemination of his works as a contribution to literature.

In the novel, the unnamed hero lives in social isolation and "dissociates himself in his capacity as a creative artist" (Buttry 228). He does not consider himself part of the masses and he communicates only with a few people to support his needs and self-expression. He is described as an outsider and unclassed young man who willingly adopts this outcast status. His isolation and sensitivity are increased by his starvation and extreme poverty in the city. "Intet undgik min Opmærksomhed, jeg var klar og aandsnærværende, alle Ting strømmed ind paa mig med en skinnende Tydelighed, som om der pludselig var bleven et stærkt Lys omkring mig" (Hamsun, *Sult* 19).[38] His insistence on preserving his aesthetic concerns and self-expression in his writings is confronted by financial necessity. His experience as an outcast artist is highly individualistic and graphic at

---

38 "Nothing escaped my attention, I was lucid and self-possessed, and everything rushed in upon me with a brilliant distinctness as if an intense light had suddenly sprung up around me" (Hamsun, *Hunger* 14).

times, paving the way for insight into the human soul and psyche. This personal outlook and experience in all its details helps the reader think about the modern individual fading into the masses in the city novel as one of the main forms of modernist writing. Hamsun's obsessive concern with his innovative artistic production, and the disconnection of Hamsun's hero from the city dwellers are part of artistic emancipation. His self-imposed isolation and quest for real art are realised and practiced in Kristiania, allowing for artistic voyage into new literature. In "The Cities of Modernism", Malcolm Bradbury suggests that "realism humani[s]es, naturalism scienti[s]es but [m]odernism plurali[s]es, and surreali[s]es" (Bradbury and McFarlaine 99). Experiences and unique perceptions of the modern artist are encapsulated in the spirit of the culture-capital, modern societies and cultural exchanges, along with the chaos and abyss produced therein. Modernist writing, in this sense, frees the writer from earlier conventional forms and techniques, and allows for a subjective view of life expressed with a poetic/lyrical mode/language.

The city in *Sult* is an experimental space in which the starving artist ventures to his limits in terms of literary creativity and production in poverty. Throughout the narrative, the wanderings of Hamsun's hero in the streets of Kristiania make reference to the city as "a labyrinth without exit" due to his fruitless efforts to find shelter and food as an outsider (Rees 91). He is regarded as a stranger due to his different accent, yet he maintains a contempt for the Norwegian bourgeois society since he considers himself superior to the ordinary man as an artist.[39] His starvation, impoverishment and degradation only increase his disdain for others as he believes he deserves a better life. With his "self-contradiction and inconsistency", he represents a "social misfit or even anti-hero" against the city's hard-working and faithful middle-class and he is ironic about both his own condition and the city dwellers (94). His outcast status, poverty and starvation in the city also allow for a process of self-discovery in an unconventional sense as he observes the profound effects of starvation on his body and mind, invents fictional roles, lies, and tries to write articles

---

39 Harald Naess argues that *Sult* "involves both a revolt against bourgeois society [...] and a lack of interest in its improvement through social reform. It demonstrates a total subjectivity" (309).

in this condition. The city, as a labyrinth in this sense, is an experimental place for the artist's observation of his self-consciousness, pushing him to the limits of his artistic production as a means of his wilful choice for survival.[40] Often dismissed from parks and cemeteries where he tries to write an article or simply waits for inspiration, the narrator is determined to stay in the city until he loses all hope of survival by writing. His departure from the city does not promise a solution to his problems in the future, however, it marks a change in his method of resistance to the conditions he is in.

Kristiania is primarily introduced as a "strange city" that has a profound impact on the outcast writer in the opening chapter of the novel: "Det var i den Tid, jeg gik omkring og sulted i Kristiania, denne forunderlige By, som ingen forlader, før han har fået Mærker af den" (Hamsun, *Sult* 1).[41] The novel is described by Lyngstad as "an urban novel, whose action takes place within a distinctive setting of streets, squares and residential areas familiar to Kristiania residents" (223). The city as an urban space plays a significant role in "shap[ing] the narrative structure" of the novel (Moretti 8). The experiences of Hamsun's hero are considerably shaped by the place he inhabits. The strolling of the protagonist through "the grey streets of an impersonal big city, utterly alone in his struggle to survive, both physically and spiritually", turns his attention to himself and his sensations rather than his surroundings (Buttry 27). Trying to write his articles in open spaces, he is unable to concentrate because "de forskelligste Tingunderlige Paafund, Luner, Indfald af min urolige Hjærne" (Hamsun, *Sult* 4–5).[42] Since he is "rootless, without friends, denuded of objects", he

---

40 Freud writes: "It has struck me that in many of what are known as 'psychological' novels only one person—once again the hero—is described from within. The author sits inside his mind, as it were, and looks at the other characters from out- side. The psychological novel in general no doubt owes its special nature to the inclination of the modern writer to split up his ego, by self-observation, into many part egos, and in consequence, to personify the currents of his own mental life in several heroes" (see Lodge 40).

41 "It was in those days when I wandered about hungry in Kristiania, that strange city which no one leaves before it has set mark upon him" (Hamsun, *Hunger* 3).

42 "strange whimsies, moods, caprices of my restless brain" (Hamsun, *Hunger* 5).

keeps moving in the streets of the city and is sometimes forced to move because his presence creates suspicion, a deviance in urban space (Auster 254). The difficulty of finding shelter bewilders him and leads to an existential crisis linked with inhabitation and places when he asks: "Hvor skulde jeg dog gøre af mig? Et Sted maatte jeg jo være" (Hamsun, *Sult* 64).[43] It also refers to the absence of a place in the city that could tolerate his survival on his own terms: "Jeg agted ikke at synke, sammen, jeg vilde dø staaende" (315).[44] The city acts as a hostile labyrinth that he is caught in but he cannot return home because he does not feel he belongs to any specific place.

---

43 "Where was I to go? I had to be somewhere, after all" (Hamsun, *Hunger* 43).
44 "I had no intention of collapsing, I would die on my feet!" (Hamsun, *Hunger* 207).

7. Conclusion: A Comparative Outlook

The plot structures of *New Grub Street* and *Mai ve Siyah* are complex and interwoven with subplots on the portrayal of the literary networks of men of letters and the publishing culture in late-nineteenth-century England and the Ottoman Empire. In the two novels, the sequence of events presents a cause-and-effect relation and it functions as a means of creating a realistic representation of the artist's struggle and ultimate failure to adapt to the changing mode of the literary market and its demands. The subplots display the conflicting views of the protagonist with those of professional writers, critics and publishers who regard literature as a business. The novels also consist of a subtle introduction, rising action, climax, falling action and closure in the conventional sense. A third-person narrative is used in both. The hopes and dreams of the protagonists gradually diminish with the unexpected problems they encounter and through their passive resistance to conforming to the transforming world. Their private life is also intensely affected by their degrading conditions and they lose their loved ones towards the end of the narratives.

In terms of differences in the structure, Gissing first introduces Jasper ("A Man of His Day"), the Yule family and then Reardon ("An Author and his Wife"), whilst Halit Ziya presents Ahmet Cemil on a night he is celebrating the newspaper with other writers, the editor and proprietor. The contrast between the protagonists and other characters in the novels is presented through their relations, motivations and goals in the first chapters. The presence of Jasper, Alfred and Marian Yule, Whelpdale and Biffen in *New Grub Street*, and Raci and other writers in the newspaper in *Mai ve Siyah* exemplify these contradictory views in the period. Gissing maintains a more balanced share in the flow of events between different characters, whose personal views on the transforming literary market are equally shared by an objective narrative voice; Halit Ziya's narrative is mainly focused on Ahmet Cemil's experiences and personal views on art and literary production as the poet-protagonist and contrasting views are presented with a critical approach. One reason for Gissing's technique might be the three-volume-format, which required lengthy descriptions,

dialogues and subplots in prose of the period. The mode of literary production, in this sense, clearly had an effect on the formation of the plot.
The temporal structures of the novels are also distinctive since the chro-
nological order of events is linear in Gissing's novel, whilst it is nonlinear
in the narrative of Halit Ziya, with shifts from past to present regarding
Ahmet Cemil's childhood years and memories.

Sult is an artist's novel as well but it has significant differences in terms of
its plot structure and presentation of the literary production in Kristiania.
The plot structure is simpler than that of New Grub Street and Mai ve
Siyah, and it denies a cause-and-effect relationship. Each section seems
disconnected and there is a perpetual cycle of starvation, wandering and
the effort of writing articles. The protagonist is a solitary artist and literary circles are not presented in the narrative, except in his frequent visits
to newspapers and editors to discuss the publication of his essays. In this
respect, the novel presents an individualistic and subjective portrayal of
the artist estranged and isolated from not only society but also the literary
world. The narrative does not contain a traditional plot or structure, either;
there is no information about the central character in the first chapter, a
first-person narrative is used, and instead of a climax, rising and falling
action, there is a fluctuating flow of everyday life. The moments of extreme
starvation, poverty and the changing mood of the character give the work
a surreal quality. Like in Mai ve Siyah, seasons mirror the gradual degradation and loss of hope in his struggles. In the endings, Reardon and Biffen
die, while Ahmet Cemil and Hamsun's hero decide to leave the city for a
new life. Each character makes a different choice, yet their struggles and
failures in the city are mutual.

The authors' choice of title for their novels, on the other hand, reveal
a symbolic attribution to the corruption of the literary market and the
publication world in various ways. New Grub Street reflects the writer's
criticism of the changing modes of literary production from the eighteenth
to the late nineteenth century and a call for attention to the devaluation
of artistic creation and authorship in England. Halit Ziya chooses colours
to symbolise the dreams (blue) and disappointments (black) of an aspiring
young writer and poet in the period in Istanbul. Hamsun's title is also carefully selected since the author uses the effects of starvation and impoverishment on the artist's body and mind, as well as his literary production, and

draws attention to the intimate link between money and artistic creation. The detrimental influence of financial concerns on aesthetic concerns is emphasised through hunger, as a real and simultaneously symbolic term. The titles of the three novels, in this regard, are deliberate and thoughtful choices by Gissing, Hamsun and Halit Ziya in order to underline the need for artistic freedom and independence without any economic concerns.

Although the literary histories, economic, political and socio-cultural features of late-nineteenth-century England, Norway and the Ottoman Empire differ to a great extent, the condition of the artist caught between aesthetic and economic concerns reveals significant similarities. The literary ideals of the authors in the novels are profoundly affected by the financial difficulties they go through and their uncompromising attitudes to the changing publishing market aggravate their situation and lead to extreme impoverishment. Reardon is unable to write the three-decker novels that would appeal to the public taste, the publishers and Mudie's library and he faces poverty and separation from his wife as a result of his financial problems; Ahmet Cemil translates cheap popular novels, tutors a child and writes essays on popular subjects for the newspaper in order to look after his family, although he only wishes to write poetry; Hamsun's starving artist strolls the streets looking for a way to write articles for publication since his survival depends upon the few kroners he will receive from the editors. These conditions raise fundamental questions about the role of money in artistic production, creativity and ideals.

Although conditions of creativity are often associated with a number of variable factors in the scholarship, these novels place a great deal of importance on the impact of basic needs not being satisfied on artistic production. Neither Reardon nor Hamsun's hero are able to make a particular contribution in their extreme poverty and the quality of their works is evaluated based on publishers' criterions and the public demand. Ahmet Cemil's poetry is also considered a failure due to Raci's criticism in his literary circle. At this point, lack of fulfilment of basic needs and comfort suggests a decline in artistic production and creativity. However, it is also possible that their contemporaries are devoid of an understanding of original contributions since they are so concerned with the demands of the public, editors and publishers. The author's economic needs strongly constrain their choice of plot, subject and form in their productions, as well as their originality and creativity. The anxiety and stress originating from economic concerns therefore often results in a decline in aesthetic concerns or artistic creativity.

From a different perspective, as artist's novels, these narratives are original contributions to literature partly due to the self-portrait of the artist who is caught between the contradictions of the period. The autobiographical details give them the qualities of a *meta-novel* or *Künstlerroman* and represent the distinctive features of the literary culture in the period. In particular, implicit and explicit forms of censorships are represented in a realist manner and their influence on the character's literary production is elaborated in detail. In Gissing's novel, the public opinion and the effects of Mudie's library are emphasised; in Halit Ziya's novel state censorship and self-censorship practices are elaborated; and in Hamsun's novel the editor's demands are strongly connected to the middle-class values and readers' demands. It is observed that both prior and post censorship, and implicit and explicit forms of censorship lead to self-censorship in the translation process, novel writing and the publication of articles in newspapers and journals. They play a major role as restrictive forces, whilst sometimes triggering creativity to find alternative types of transgression in artistic production. The presence and publication of these novels, on the other hand, exemplifies the persistence of creative writers in the production of idealistic works despite obvious obstructions.

In terms of characterisation, the writers' personal traits and creativity, there are a number of critical aspects to be considered. Reardon's introversion, sensitivity, self-discipline, subjectivity, insight and imagination are accompanied by stress, anxiety, non-conformity and a lack of intrinsic motivation. Conversely, Jasper's openness to experience, overexcitability, resilience, risk-taking, motivation for work, ambition for fame and self-promotion, confidence and objectivity help him find a place in the new literary market. Reardon's lack of motivation, perseverance and risk tolerance hinders his progress in artistic creativity in the changing conditions of the period. Ahmet Cemil is a creative writer and poet whose imagination, intuition, passion for work, perceptiveness, volition and values help him compose his new poetry, whilst he is affected by anxiety, stress, daydreaming and over-sensitivity. His delights in creative endeavour are impacted by his deteriorating family life, financial problems and continuous toil. He has a life with a purpose; however, the flow of events leads him to give up on his ideals and creativity. Unlike Reardon and Ahmet Cemil, Hamsun's hero is endowed with some features of creative artists, such as overexcitability, intense sensitivity, perceptiveness, resilience, risk-taking, self-efficacy, tolerance for ambiguity, deviance, independence, non-conformity, impulsivity, playfulness, confidence and subjectivity. These characteristics add dynamism into the narrative structure and a modernist perspective to the process of artistic production. The personal traits of these characters reflect some similar aspects to those of their writers; however, they also represent a class of young intellectuals/authors striving for a deserved place in the literary world in their specific temporal and spatial contexts.

Regarding the relationship between the city and literary production, the settings of these novels draw our attention to the impact of urban space on artistic production, censorship and livelihoods. In the late nineteenth century, London, Oslo and İstanbul all had distinctive socio-economic and political conditions in which the artist had to maintain his/her art and survival in better living conditions than the poor. London and Istanbul were more developed cities than Oslo in the period, yet the artists' experiences do not seem to reflect the widening gap between these cities. In the novels, the names of real streets or places are used as representations of literary production in the city. The British Museum in London and the Babiâli Street in Istanbul are specific locations for artistic production and publication. In *Sult*, such a specific place is not referred to but the public parks and streets Hamsun's hero wanders all day present realistic representations of the city. The unclassed and emigrant position of the hero might relate to this representation. Reardon and Ahmet Cemil live in the conditions of a lower-middle-class family, therefore their homes are also close to the respective literary centres. When Reardon's economic condition worsens, he moves to Croydon, occupied by the lower classes. All these specific places are realistic representations of the transforming literary market and the influence of urban space on individuals, who are estranged from the society they write for.

8. References

"A Brief History of the Private Press Movement." *Oxenbridge Press*, https://oxenbridgepress.co.uk/a-brief-history-of-the-private-press-movement/ Accessed 23 March 2020.

"Basın Dünyasının Hafızası: Babıâli." *Fikriyat Dergisi*, 7 September 2018, https://www.fikriyat.com/kultur-sanat/2018/09/07/basin-dunyasinin-hafizasi-babili. Accessed 30 April 2020.

"*Cambridge Dictionary.*" Cambridge University Press, 2020, https://dictionary.cambridge.org/tr/sözlük/ingilizce/self-censorship. Accessed 3 March 2020.

"En Ny Allmanach paa det Aar efter Jesu Christi Fødsel 1644. Christiania Aff Tyge Nielssøn." *National Library of Norway* https://www.nb.no/items/1cbb5737ed0ec7c6dad78e6676c4ddba?page=0&searchText=Tyge%20Nielss%C3%B8n. Accessed 12 December 2019.

"George Gissing, 'New Grub Street', 1891." The University of Iowa, http://myweb.uiowa.edu/fsboos/questions/gissinggrub.htm Accessed 21 April 2020

"The Atlas of Early Printing." *University of Iowa.* http://atlas.lib.uiowa.edu. Accessed 3 January 2020.

Albin, Verónica. "On Censorship: A Conversation with Ilan Stavans." *Translation Journal, vol.* 9, no. 3, 2005, https://translationjournal.net/journal/33censorship1.htm. Accessed 12 November 2019.

Arata, Stephen, editor. Introduction. *New Grub Street*, by George Gissing, Ontario, Broadview Editions, 2007.

Auster, Paul. "The Art of Hunger." *Hunger, by* Knut Hamsun, Edinburgh, Canongate Books, 2011, pp. 249–261.

Ayaydın Cebe, Günil Özlem. *19. Yüzyılda Osmanlı Toplumu ve Basılı Türkçe Edebiyat: Etkileşimler, Değişimler, Çeşitlilik.* 2009. Bilkent Üniversitesi, PhD Dissertation.

Bateson, P., and P. Martin. *Oyun, Oyunbazlık, Yaratıcılık ve İnovasyon.* Translated by Songül Kırgezen, İstanbul, Ayrıntı Yayınları, 2014.

Baykal, Erol. *The Ottoman Press, 1908–1923*. 2013. Cambridge University, PhD Dissertation.

Ben-Ari, Nitsa. "When Literary Censorship Is Not Strictly Enforced, Self-Censorship Rushes." *TTR*, vol. 23, no. 2, 2010, pp. 133–166. https://doi.org/10.7202/1009163ar Accessed 10 February 2020

Benjamin, Walter. *Pasajlar*. Translated by Ahmet Cemal, İstanbul, YKY, 2001.

Borgna, E. *Melankoli*. Translated by Meryem Mine Çilingiroğlu, İstanbul, Yapı Kredi Yayınları, 2014.

Bourdieu, Pierre. *Language and Symbolic Power*. Cambridge, Polity Press, 1992.

Bourdieu, Pierre. *On Television*. Translated by Priscilla Parkhurst Ferguson, The New Press, 1998.

Boyd, Julia. "Literary Fascists of the 1930s, Great and Small." *Literary Hub*, 2 August 2018, https://lithub.com/literary-fascists-of-the-1930s-great-and-small

Bradbury, Malcolm. "The Cities of Modernism." *Modernism 1890 1930*, edited by Malcolm Bradbury and James McFarlane, London, Penguin Books, 1991.

Brake, Laurel. " 'The Trepidation of the Spheres': Serials and Books in the Nineteenth Century." *Print in Transition, 1850–1910: Studies in Media and Book History*. Basingstoke, Palgrave, 2001, pp. 3–26.

Burt, Richard. "(Un)censoring in Detail: The Fetish of Censorship in the Early Modern Past and the Postmodern Present." *Censorship and Silencing: Practices of Cultural Regulation*, edited by Robert C. Post. Los Angeles, Getty Research Institute for the History of Art and the Humanities, 1998, pp. 17–42

Butler, Judith. "Ruled Out: Vocabularies of the Censor." *Censorship and Silencing: Practices of Cultural Regulation*, edited by Robert C. Post. Los Angeles, The Getty Research Institute for the History of Art and the Humanities, 1998, pp. 247–259.

Butler, Judith. *Excitable Speech. A Politics of the Performative*. New York, Routledge, 1997.

Buttry, Dolores. "Down and out in Paris, London, and Oslo: Pounding the Pavement with Knut Hamsun and and George Orwell." *Comparative Literature Studies*, vol. 25, no. 3, 1988, pp. 225–241.

Chapman, James. "Norway and the Nazis." *Censorship: A World Encyclopaedia*, vol. 3, edited by D. Jones, London, 2001, p. 1740.

Çıkla, Selçuk. "Tanzimat'tan Günümüze Gazete-Edebiyat İlişkisi." *Türkbilig*, vol. 18, 2009, pp. 34–63.

Clegg, Cyndia Susan. *Censorship*, 2012, https://www. oxfordbibliographies.com/view/document/obo-9780199846719/obo-9780199846719-0011.xml. Accessed 2 January 2020.

Coughie, John, editor. *Theories of Authorship*. London, Routledge, 2001.

Dahl, Gina. *Book Collections of Clerics in Norway, 1650–1750*. Leiden/Boston, Brill, 2010.

Deal, Laura. *Zola in England: Controversy and Change in the 1890s*. 2008. American University, PhD Dissertation.

Demirkol, Neslihan. *1850–1900 Yılları Arasında Edebiyat Yayıncılığı Alanının Yeniden Biçimlenmesi ve Edebiyat Çevirileri Piyasasının Doğuşu*. 2015. Bilkent Universitesi, PhD Dissertation.

Downs, B. W. *Modern Norwegian Literature 1860–1918*. Cambridge, Cambridge UP, 1966.

Doyle, Andrew. "Self-censorship is the Enemy of Creativity." 10 December 2019, https://www.spiked-online.com/2019/12/10/self-censorship-is-the-enemy-of-creativity/ Accessed 5 March 2020.

Ducas, Slyvie. "Authors: Censorship and Self-Censorship." *Ethnologie Française*, vol. 36 no. 1, 2016, pp. 111–119.

Duman, H. *Osmanlı-Türk Süreli Yayınları ve Gazeteleri Bibliyografyası ve Toplu Kataloğu: 1828–1928, I-II*. Ankara, Enformasyon ve Dokümantasyon Hizmetleri Vakfı Yayınları, 2000.

Eliot, Simon. "Aspects of the Victorian Book." *The British Library*, 2013, http://www.bl.uk/collections/early/victorian/pu_intro.html. Accessed 10 February 2020.

Erkul Yağcı, Ahu Selin. *Turkey's Reading (R)Evolution A Study on Books, Readers and Translation (1840–1940)*. 2012. Boğaziçi Üniversitesi, PhD Dissertation.

Evin, Ahmet Ö. *Türk Romanının Kökenleri ve Gelişimi*. İstanbul, Agora Kitaplığı, 2004.

Feltes, N. N. *Literary Capital and the Late Victorian Novel*. Madison, University of Madison Press, 1993.

Ferguson, Robert. *Enigma: The Life of Knut Hamsun.* London, Hutchinson, 1987.

Finn, R. P. *Türk Romanı/ İlk Dönem, 1872–1900,* Translated by Tomris Uyar, İstanbul, Agora Kitaplığı, 2003.

Foerstel, Herbert N., editor. *Banned in the USA: A Reference Guide to Book Censorship in Schools and Public Libraries.* Westport, Greenwood Press, 2006.

Freshwater, Helen. "Towards a Redefinition of Censorship." *Censorship and Cultural Regulation in the Modern Age,* edited by Beate Müller. Amsterdam, Rodopi, 2004, pp. 225–245.

Gettmann, Royal A. *A Victorian Publisher: A Study of the Bentley Papers.* Cambridge, Cambridge UP, 1960.

Ghazaryan, Almina. "The National Museum of Denmark." *Type and Press,* 4 January 2017, http://typeand.press/new-blog/2017/1/4/the-national-museum-of-denmark?rq=Denmark. Accessed 24 December 2019.

Gissing, George. *Charles Dickens: A Critical Study.* Dodd, Mead, 1898.

Gissing, George. *New Grub Street.* Oxford, Oxford University Press, 1998.

Gökşen, Bahanur Garan. *Şairin Romani, Romanin Şiiri: Tanzimat'tan Cumhuriyet'e Türk Romaninda Şair ve Şiir.* 2018. Mimar Sinan Güzel Sanatlar Üniversitesi, PhD Dissertation.

Goldstein, Robert Justin. "Political Theatre Censorship in Nineteenth-Century France in Comparative European Perspective", *European History Quarterly,* vol. 40, no. 2, 2010, pp. 240–265.

Goldstein, Robert Justin. *Political Censorship of the Arts and the Press in Nineteenth-Europe.* UK, Palgrave Macmillan, 1989.

Good, John, editor. Introduction. *New Grub Street,* by George Gissing, Oxford: Oxford University Press, 1993.

Griest, Guinevere L. *Mudie's Circulating Library and the Victorian Novel.* Bloomington, Indiana UP, 1970.

Güher Erer, Nadide. "A Short History of Copyright in the West, in the Ottoman Empire and in Turkey." *Türk Kütüphaneciliği,* vol. 28, no. 4, 2014, pp. 638–644.

Hague, Angela. *Fiction, Intuition and Creativity.* USA, The Catholic University of America, 2003.

Hamsun, Knut. *Briefe*. Munich, Langen-Müller, 1957.

Hamsun, Knut. *Hunger*. Translated by George Egerton, London, Leonard Smithers, 1899.

Hamsun, Knut. *Hunger*. Translated by George Egerton, New York, Alfred A. Knopf, 1920.

Hamsun, Knut. *Hunger*. Translated by Robert Bly, New York, Farrar, Straus and Giroux, 1967.

Hamsun, Knut. *Hunger*. Translated by Sverre Lyngstad, Edinburg, Canongate Books. 2011.

Hamsun, Knut. *Sult*. Copenhagen, Philipsens Forlag, 1890.

Harputlu Shah, Zeynep. "Passive Resistance in George Gissing's 'New Grub Street' and Knut Hamsun's 'Sult.'" *Nordic Journal of English Studies*, vol. 18, no. 1, 2019, pp. 95–120.

Harrison, Debbie, editor. About the Author. *Workers in the Dawn*, by George Gissing, Brighton, Victorian Secrets, 2010.

Haynes, Christine. *Lost Illusions: The Politics of Publishing in Nineteenth-Century France*. Cambridge, Harvard University Press, 2010.

Heiler, L. "Against Censorship: Literature, Transgression, and Taboo from a Diachronic Perspective." *Taboo and Transgression in British Literature from the Renaissance to the Present*, edited by S. Horlacher, S Glomb, and L. Heiler, New York, Palgrave Macmillan, 2010, pp. 49–71.

Hennesey, Beth A. and Teresa M. Amabile. "Conditions of Creativity." *The Nature of Creativity*, edited by R. Sternberg, Cambridge, Cambridge UP, 1988, pp. 11–43.

Houghton, Walter J. *The Victorian Frame of Mind 1830–1870*. New Haven, Yale UP, 1957.

Humpál, Martin. *The Roots of Modernist Narrative: Knut Hamsun's Novels "Hunger", "Mysteries," and "Pan."* Austin, The University of Texas, 1996.

Huyugüzel, Ömer Faruk. *Halit Ziya Uşaklıgil*. Ankara, Akçay Yayınları, 2010.

Huyugüzel, Ömer Faruk. *Hüseyin Cahit Yalçın'ın Hayatı ve Edebî Eserleri Üzerinde Bir Araştırma*. İzmir, Ege Üniversitesi Edebiyat Fakültesi Yayınları, 1984.

İskit, Server. *Türkiye'de Matbuat İdareleri ve Politikaları.* Ankara, Basın ve Yayım Umum Müdürlüğü, 1943.

İşli, Nedret. "Bab-ı Âli'de Yayınevleri." *Bolsohays News,* October 2011, http://www.bolsohays.com/yazar-98/babilide-ermeni-kitapcilar.html

James, Henry. "The Future of the Novel: Essays on the Art of Fiction," *Essays on the Art of Fiction,* edited by Leon Edel, New York, Vintage, 1956.

Johnson, Samuel. "Grubstreet." 1755, *A Dictionary of the English Language: A Digital Edition of the 1755 Classic by Samuel Johnson,* edited by Brand Besalke, https://johnsonsdictionaryonline.com/grubstreet/ Accessed 5 March 2020

Kaplan, Mehmet. "'Mai ve Siyah' Romanının Üslûbu Hakkında." *Türk Edebiyatı Üzerine Araştırmalar I,* 1976, pp. 437–458.

Kaplan, Mehmet. *Türk Edebiyatı Üzerine Araştırmalar I.* İstanbul, Dergâh Yayınları, 2009.

Kerman, Zeynep, and Ömer Faruk Huyugüzel. "Halit Ziya Uşaklıgil Bibliyografyası." *Türk Dili,* Ankara, no. 529, 1996, pp. 164–248.

Kilgour, Frederick. *The Evolution of the Book.* New York, Oxford University Press, 1998.

Kittang, Atle. "Knut Hamsun's 'Sult': Psychological Deep Structures and Metapoetic Plot." *Facets of European Modernism,* edited by Janet Gorton, Norwich, University of East Anglia, 1985, pp. 295–308.

Kılıç Gündoğdu, Ayşen. *Mai ve Siyah Romanında Tasvirler ve Yüklendiği Foksiyonlar.* 2009. Adnan Menderes University, MA Dissertation.

Kolcu, Ali İhsan. *Türkçe'de Batı Şiiri.* Erzurum, Salkımsöğüt Yayınevi, 2008.

Kolloen, Ingar S. *Knut Hamsun: Dreamer and Dissenter.* Translated by Deborah Dawkin and Erik Skuggevik. New Haven, Yale University Press, 2009.

Kundera, Milan. "Comedy is Everywhere." *Index on Censorship,* vol. 6, no. 6, 1977, pp. 3–7.

Lamarque, Peter. *The Philosophy of Literature.* Malden, Blackwell, 2009.

Larsen, Lars Frode. *Knut Hamsun: The Author and His Times.* Norwegian Heritage, Font, 2012.

Lâtug, Diana. "An Overview of Knut Hamsun's Perception in the Romanian Cultural Printed Press." *Nordlit*, no. 38, 2016, pp. 52–66.

Laursen, John Christian. "Journal of Modern European History." *Censorship in Early Modern Europe*, vol. 3, no. 1, 2005, pp. 100–121.

Law, Graham. " 'A Vile Way of Publishing': Gissing and Serials." *Victorian Review*, vol. 33, no. 1, 2007, pp. 71–86.

Law, Graham. *Serializing Fiction in the Victorian Press*. Hampshire, Palgrave, 2000.

Lieberman, Sima. *Norwegian Population Growth in the 19th Century, Economy and History*, vol. 11, no. 1, 1968, pp. 52–66.

Lyngstad, Sverre. Translator's Trap: Knut Hamsun's 'Hunger' in English. *Hunger*, by Knut Hamsun, Edinburg: Canongate Books, 2011, pp. 219–236.

Mattheisen, Paul E, Arthur C. Young and Pierre Coustillas, editors. *The Collected Letters of George Gissing*. 9 vols. Athens, Ohio University Press, 1990–97.

Matthew Selwyn, "Review: Hunger by Knut Hamsun." *Bibliofreak*, 30 January 2013, https://www.bibliofreak.net/2013/01/review-hunger-by-knut-hamsun.html

McFarlane, James. "The Mind of Modernism." *Modernism 1890–1930*, edited by Malcolm Bradbury and James McFarlane. London, Penguin Books, 1991, pp. 80–96.

Menke, Richard. "The End of the Three-Volume Novel System, 27 June 1894.", 2013 *BRANCH: Britain, Representation and Nineteenth-Century History*, edited by Dino Franco Felluga, *Extension of Romanticism and Victorianism on the Net*. https://www. branchcollective.org/?ps_articles=richard-menke-the-end-of-the-three-volume-novel-system-27-june-1894 Accessed 13 December 2019

Mill, John Stuart. "On Liberty." *The Collected Works of John Stuart Mill*, edited by John M. Robson, London, Routledge, 1977, Vol, XVIII, pp. 213–310

Moore, George. *Confessions of a Young Man*. London, Heinemann, 1933.

Moore, Nicole. "Censorship." *North American Literatures, Film, TV and Media, Cultural Studies*, 2016, https://oxfordre.com/

literature/view/10.1093/acrefore/9780190201098.001.0001/acrefore-
9780190201098-e-71?mediaType=Article&result=1&rskey=1KJWVb.
Accessed 12 October 2019.

Moore, Nicole. *Censorship and the Limits of the Literary: A Global View.* New York, Bloomsbury, 2015.

Morton, Peter. "A Review on George Gissing's Letters." *The Victorian Web*, 2004, http://www.victorianweb.org/authors/gissing/letters.html. Accessed 4 May 2020.

Naess, Harald S. *Norwegian Literary Bibliography, 1956–1970.* Univ.-Forl, 1975.

Negri A., and M. Sironi. "Censorship of the Visual Arts in Italy 1815–1915." *Political Censorship of the Visual Arts in Nineteenth-Century Europe*, edited by R. J. Goldstein R.J. and A.M. Nedd. London, Palgrave Macmillan, 2015, pp. 191–219.

Nesta, Frederic. *The Commerce of Literature: George Gissing and Late Victorian Publishing, 1880–1903.* 2007. University of Wales, PhD Dissertation.

Nesta, Frederic. "The Myth of the 'The Triple Headed Monster': Economics of the Three-Volume Novel." *Publishing History*, vol. 61, 2007, pp. 47–69.

Newth, Mette. "The Long History of Censorship." *Beacon for Freedom of Expression*, 2010, http://www.beaconforfreedom.org/liste. html?tid=415. Accessed 30 November 2019.

O'Leary, Catherine, Diego Santos Sánchez, and Michael Thompson, editors. *Global Insights on Theatre Censorship.* New York, Routledge, 2016.

Parla, Jale. *Türk Romanında Yazar ve Başkalaşım.* İstanbul, İletişim Yayınları, 2012.

Parlatır, İsmail. "Halit Ziya Uşaklıgil." *Türk Dili,* vol. 529, 1996, pp. 87–89.

Patterson, Annabel. *Censorship and Interpretation: The Conditions of Writing and Reading in Early Modem England.* Wisconsin, University of Wisconsin Press, 1984.

Patterson, Anthony. "Making Mrs Grundy's Flesh Creep: George Egerton's Assault on Late-Victorian Censorship." *Victoriographies*, vol. 3, no. 1, 2013, pp. 64–77.

Petersen, Teddy K. "Norway." *Censorship: A World Encyclopedia,* vol. 3, edited by Derek Jones, London, Routledge, 2001, pp. 1738–1741.

Petersen, Teddy K. "Norway" and "Since 1945." *Censorship: A World Encyclopedia,* vol. 3, edited by D. Jones London, 2001, pp. 1738–1739.

Piirto, Jane. "The Personalities of Creative Writers." *The Psychology of Creative Writing,* edited by S.B. Kaufman and J. C. Kaufman, Delhi, Cambridge UP, 2009, pp. 3–22

Pilgrim, Anne. "Censored Metaphor in 'Demos.' " *The Gissing Newsletter,* vol. 7, no. 1, 1971, pp. 9–11.

Piper, Andrew. *Dreaming in Books: The Making of the Bibliographic Imagination in the Romantic Age.* London, University of Chicago, 2009.

Poole, Adrian. *Gissing in Context.* London, Macmillan, 1975.

Pope, Rob and Joan Swann. Introduction. *Creativity in Language and Literature,* edited by Pope Swann and R. Carter, New York, Palgrave Macmillan, 2011.

Post, Robert C., editor. *Censorship and Silencing: Practices of Cultural Regulation.* Los Angeles, The Getty Research Institute for the History of Art and the Humanities, 1998.

Rees, Daniel. *Hunger and Modern Writing: Melville, Kafka, Hamsun and Wright.* 2015. Ludwig-Maximilians-Universität Munich, PhD Dissertation.

Rose, Mark. *Authors and Owners: The Invention of Copyright.* Cambridge, Harvard UP, 1993.

Rossi, Riikka. "The Everyday in Nordic Modernism: Knut Hamsun's 'Sult' and Maria Jotuni's 'Arkielämää.' " *Scandinavian Studies, vol.* 82, no. 4, 2010, pp. 417–438.

Ruud, M. B. 1916. "Knut Hamsun." *Publications of the Society for the Advancement of Scandinavian Study,* vol. 3, no. 3, 1916, pp. 241–252.

Samier, Henri. *Intuition, Creativity, Innovation,* USA, ISTE and John Wiley, 2018.

Saunders, David. "Copyright and the Legal Relations of Literature." *New Formations,* no. 4, 1988, pp. 125–143.

Sejersted, Francis. "A Theory of Economic and Technological Development in Norway in the Nineteenth Century." *Scandinavian Economic History Review*, vol. 40, no. 1, 1992, pp. 40–75.

Serdar, Ali, and Reyhan Tutumlu Serdar. "Tradition of Serial Novels in Ottoman/Turkish Literature." *ATINER's Conference Paper* Series, LIT2014-1239, 2014, pp. 3–12.

Severn, Stephen E. "The Quasi-Professional Culture, Conservative Ideology, and the Narrative Structure of George Gissing's 'New Grub Street.'" *Journal of Narrative Theory*, vol. 40, no. 2, 2010, pp. 156–188.

Showalter, Elaine. "Sexual Anarchy: Gender and Culture at the Fin De Siècle." 29 Aug 1991, https://www.amazon.com.au/Sexual-Anarchy-Gender-Culture-Siecle/dp/0140115870

Stark, Gary. *Banned in Berlin: Literary Censorship in Imperial Germany, 1871–1918*. Berghahn Books, 2012.

Storr, Anthony. *The Dynamics of Creation*. Virginia, Penguin Books, 1991.

Tanpınar, Ahmet Hamdi. *Halit Ziya Uşaklıgil, Edebiyat Üzerine Makaleler*. İstanbul, Dergâh Yayınevi, 1995.

The Cambridge Handbook of Literary Authorship, edited by Ingo Berensmeyer, Gert Buelens, and Marysa Demoor. Cambridge, Cambridge UP, 2019.

The Encyclopedia of the Novel, edited by Peter Melville Logan, UK, Wiley and Blackwell, 2011.

Thomas, Donald Serrell. *A Long Time Burning; the History of Literary Censorship in England*. New York, Praeger, 1969.

Tüzer, İbrahim. "Roman Sanatı Üzerine Düşünen bir Yazar, Halit Ziya Uşaklıgil ve Poetik bir Metin olarak Hikâye." *Ayraç*, 8 Mayıs 2010.

Uçman, Abdullah. Introduction and Notes. *Kırk Yıl*, by Halit Ziya Uşaklıgil, Istanbul, YKY Yayınları, 2017, pp. 7–20.

Uşaklıgil, Halit Ziya. *Hikâye*. Istanbul, Dergâh Yayınları, 2018.

Uşaklıgil, Halit Ziya. *Kırk Yıl*. Istanbul, YKY Yayınları, 2017.

Uşaklıgil, Halit Ziya. *Mai ve Siyah*. Istanbul, Can Yayınları, 2016.

Uysal, Zeynep. *Metruk Ev/Halit Ziya Romanında Modern Osmanlı Bireyi*. İstanbul, İletişim Yayınları, 2014.

Wilde, Oscar. "The Soul of Man under Socialism." 1891. https://www.
marxists.org/reference/archive/wilde-oscar/soul-man/. Accessed
20 April 2020.

Wong, Marcelle. *Censorship in Late-Nineteenth Century Britain*. 2009.
University of Edinburgh, PhD Dissertation.

Wood, James. "Addicted to Unpredictability." *London Review of
Books,* vol. 20, no. 23, 1998. https://www.lrb.co.uk/the-paper/
v20/n23/james-wood/addicted-to-unpredictability. Accessed
12 March 2020

Yosmaoğlu, İpek K. "Chasing the Printed Word: Press Censorship in
the Ottoman Empire, 1876–1913." *The Turkish Studies Association
Journal*, vol. 27, no. 1/2, 2003, pp. 15–49.

Zemer, Lior. *The Idea of Authorship in Copyright*. Hampshire,
Ashgate, 2007.